Business Culture Design

To Shannon,
I am looking forward to the journey of imagination, creativity and building ahead.

Rita J. King

Dr. Simon Sagmeister is founder of The Culture Institute, Zurich, and Partner for Culture Development at Science House, New York. He combines scientific research, leadership expertise, and practical experience from working with companies around the world. Many businesses large and small, Fortune 500 companies as well as family enterprises and non-profit organizations already use the Culture Map to actively develop their corporate culture.

Simon Sagmeister

Business Culture Design

Develop Your Corporate Culture
with the Culture Map

Translated from German by Joe Paul Kroll

Campus Verlag
Frankfurt/New York

The original edition was published in 2016 by Campus Verlag with the title *Business Culture Design. Gestalten Sie Ihre Unternehmenskultur mit der Culture Map* All rights reserved.

ISBN 978-3-593-50840-5 Print
ISBN 978-3-593-43815-3 E-Book (PDF)

Cover design: Simon Sagmeister and The Collected Works, New York
Typesetting: Fotosatz L. Huhn, Linsengericht
Fonts: Minion and Sharp Sans
Printing: Beltz Grafische Betriebe GmbH, Bad Langensalza
Printed in Germany

www.campus.de

Contents

Chapter 4
Corporate Culture Management

Introduction

I will never forget the day that Dr. Simon Sagmeister first visited Science House on the recommendation of his uncle, Stefan, who is a well-known designer in New York. "My nephew has a tool that maps corporate culture," Stefan told me. I remember thinking: everybody has a tool. In working with leadership teams from large companies for over a decade now, I've seen a lot of tools. Finally, we found a time to meet when Simon was in the city. James Jorasch, who founded Science House, was busy in his office that day. I told him I'd meet with Simon and let him know how it went.

As soon as Simon sat down with me in the Imagination Room at Science House to show me his laminated, multicolored hexagons, I was intrigued. Then he started explaining how the mapping works. Each hexagon represents a different dynamic, and every organization has all seven in different proportions. Companies that are extremely consensus-driven, for example, have a large green hexagon in their map. But what if they want to bring that tendency down and bring more candor and impulsive action into their dynamics? They can grow their red hexagon in the future state. The hexagons are different sizes, and they grow and shrink depending on the organization's goals and the way people interact with each other while they are accomplishing them.

The hexagons instantly came to life in front of my eyes, and as Simon explained all seven, I could already imagine the maps of all the clients I'd ever had over the years. I knew their strengths and weaknesses, and wished I'd had such a powerful way to show them what they were and give them a chance to visualize their desired future state.

I texted James to please come down and join us immediately. James is an inventor, investor and entrepreneur, and he knows a big idea when he sees it. When Simon left, I turned to James and said, "I couldn't love that guy more."

The bell rang. It was Simon again.

"I forgot to give you this chocolate bar that I brought from Zurich," he said.

That tells you everything you need to know about the author of this book. He's brilliant, kind, provocative, and thoughtful. And he brings you chocolate.

We decided that very first day to pursue a partnership with The Culture Institute, and it's been an incredible ride in the three years that Science House has been the exclusive North American licensee of Simon Sagmeister's Culture Map system. We use it to help our clients see themselves in a completely new way, and the results, time after time, have been transformative.

Rita J. King
New York, 2018

Rita J. King is a futurist, speaker, and writer. She is the co-director of Science House New York and serves as senior advisor to The Culture Institute Zurich.

Rita works with senior leadership teams around the world to align values with business goals and advise on clear actions that trend toward the desired future culture. As a LinkedIn Influencer, she regularly inspires her 500,000 followers. Features by her or about her work have been aired on CNN and the BBC, and published in *The New York Times*, *TIME*, *Fast Company, Le Figaro, Psychology Today, Inc.*, and many more.

Chapter 1
Culture: In the Thick of Things

Corporate culture in a nutshell

"We need to make culture tangible!," my boss said to me. That was in 2004, and I remember the conversation well. "When we talk about strategy or structure, everybody knows what we're talking about right away. After all, it's right there on paper," he continued. "But when culture is at stake, all people tend to come up with are vague and vapid ideas." That company's management knows only too well how important a role culture has to play in an organization's development. Julius Blum, a global champion in the furniture industry, is still family-owned after three generations and employs more than 5,000 people. The mindset of their organization is something the owners have always taken seriously. Their corporate culture is something they never left up to chance.

They knew that for a company to be successful, corporate culture had to be managed consciously. That is why the company wanted me on board. In the process of researching my dissertation, I was to make a scientific study of how culture could be managed on a practical level. After my studies, this was my first contact with professional life, but I had already gotten to know different cultures in several internships abroad. What is more, I had subliminally experienced the way corporate culture works growing up in my parents' family business. Now it was my task to offer a theoretical description of culture that would be of practical use to the company. So far, so good. I was interested in the subject from the start. But at the time, I was not aware that it would shape my professional career to this day.

The iceberg model

Anyone who takes a closer look at the current literature on culture will soon hit an iceberg.[1] The iceberg model symbolizes the existence of various levels of culture: There are parts visible above the surface, but most of it is concealed under water and hence rather less easily spotted. It is on these hidden elements that the visible ones are built.

Applying this scheme to corporate culture, the visible manifestations are the things that can immediately be seen (and heard): How are people dressed—in shorts and t-shirts or suits and ties? Are they sitting in closed offices or an open-plan loft? What do meetings look like? And who gets the best parking spot—the boss or the most successful salesperson? Or just whoever gets there first in the morning? The first time you enter a company, you find yourself bombarded by such cultural artifacts. Facebook, for instance, greets visitors with brightly colored murals. Some desks are decorated with big, colorful balloons—they indicate an employee's anniversary. At Virgin Atlantic, you are blasted with rock music before even reaching reception. Meanwhile, BMW's symbolically freighted, cylinder-shaped head office is best accessed through its futuristic museum, BMW World.

However interesting such artifacts may be, they are merely a culture's visible symptoms, not its core. In other words, they are the tip of the iceberg. The crucial issues lie much deeper: These are the fundamental assumptions that are barely visible below the waterline. Culture is responsible for the way people perceive, think and feel, and for how they act accordingly. Yet only their actions are visible, that is, above the waterline. Their perceptions, thoughts, and feelings often lie concealed and can at best be guessed at.

What underlies these manifestations is far more difficult to recognize than the easily visible elements of culture above the waterline. Below are values, attitudes, motives, perceptions, principles, mentalities etc., and thus concepts, to define which usually requires further definitions, thus doing little to promote clarity. Maybe experts can keep them apart, but in day-to-day business dealings they tend to melt into one another. They may be discussed at length in leadership retreats and seminars, but ultimately, these cultural issues are often left hanging in the air. One may marvel at their effects and be annoyed when they ruin what objectively, logically, seemed a perfect plan.

Business Culture Design

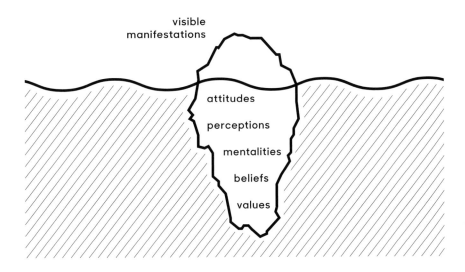

visible
manifestations

attitudes

perceptions

mentalities

beliefs

values

The concealed stratum of culture is discernible as a blur at best—much like something seen under water. It is tempting, therefore, to leave it at a superficial consideration, even though hardly anyone would dispute that such cultural elements are crucial to a business's success, especially if they suddenly rise above the surface in concrete situations: Why was the mutually agreed-upon strategy not implemented? What principles guide interactions with customers? What drives employees: speed or thoroughness? How are changes perceived: as threats or opportunities? What is the firm's attitude toward competitors? What motivates employees to push innovation forward and strive wholeheartedly for success? Everything that happens at the tip of the iceberg has its causes in the deep. Consequently, if you want to get a grip on corporate culture, you must dive under water—where the strongest driving forces of behavior can be found.

Words and deeds

In my work with different businesses, I soon came to realize that visible manifestations should not always be taken at face value. A strategy plan is an example of such a visible manifestation. All it says, however, is what people claim they want to do in the future. A strategy paper proves merely that a strategy has been formulated—no more and no less. Time will tell what ends up actually being done.

At the end of a strategy process, I have all too often witnessed how everybody seems to agree on what direction the company should take and what needs to be done. But as soon as they leave the meeting room, some participants start having niggling doubts. Sooner or later, the adage is proved right: "Culture eats strategy for breakfast!"[2] How easily culture can snatch the best-laid strategic plans and wolf them down is an experience countless businesses suffer every day: Good intentions go up in smoke, agreement turns out to be superficial, and somehow those hard-to-pin-down cultural traits below the surface make sure that nothing happens as it was supposed to.

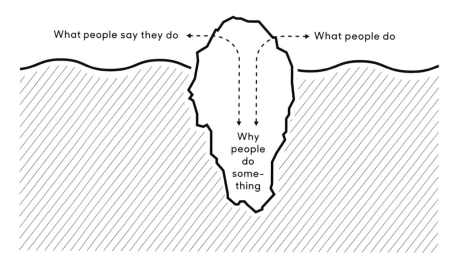

By the same token, the core values organizations publicize in their mission statements and glossy brochures often need not correspond to what their members actually do. Respect, integrity, communication, and excellence—these were the four corporate principles that Enron proclaimed prior to its criminal bankruptcy. As creditors and law-courts were later to discover, such statements may have figured in annual reports and promotional materials, but rather less so in the corporation's day-to-day activities.

Culture—but where?

Geert Hofstede, a pioneer of (business) culture research, defined culture as "the collective programming of the mind that distinguishes the members of one group or category of people from others."[3] Admittedly, "category" is not the most pleasant of terms when talking about human beings. But there also are cases of people forming a category without necessarily appearing as a coherent group. Be that as it may: Culture emerges whenever people interact. Values spread, thus producing categories of people sharing a similar "programming of the mind." In organizations, people interact intensively, which is how organizational cultures emerge. Within an organization, interaction is particularly intensive within each department. It is thus no coincidence that departmental cultures are often particularly strong. Other categories, according for instance to levels of hierarchy, local branches, or product specialization, are equally possible.

The Culture Map was designed to describe any culture that might emerge in the context of organizations. To this end, first, a so-called "System in Focus" is defined (more on this in Chapter 3). This can be an organization as a whole or just a particular part of it. It is equally possible to focus on situational patterns, on cultures, for instance, of innovation, leadership, meetings, etc.

Before reading on, take a critical look at your own corporate culture. You could also cast your mind's eye over the culture of your department. Think of a particular "System in Focus" and respond to the following statements—which apply most closely to your company or your department, and which do not apply at all? As the book goes on, your spontaneous judgments will contribute to drawing up your personal Culture Map.

	Dis-agree	Mostly dis-agree	Partly agree	Mostly agree	Agree
Our work has a positive impact on the world.	◯	◯	◯	◯	◯
We look beyond our own horizons and have the big picture in view.	◯	◯	◯	◯	◯
We strive for innovation and progress.	◯	◯	◯	◯	◯
We want to understand everything and analyze things precisely.	◯	◯	◯	◯	◯
We respect the opinions and needs of all employees.	◯	◯	◯	◯	◯
Many colleagues are like friends.	◯	◯	◯	◯	◯
We always want to win and be better than others.	◯	◯	◯	◯	◯
We pragmatically look for the best way to reach a goal.	◯	◯	◯	◯	◯
We adhere to formal hierarchies and defined processes.	◯	◯	◯	◯	◯
Pretty much everything is regulated in our company.	◯	◯	◯	◯	◯
We deal with conflicts openly and fearlessly.	◯	◯	◯	◯	◯
We act fast and boldly.	◯	◯	◯	◯	◯
Our past experience guides our decisions.	◯	◯	◯	◯	◯
We form a strong collective and stick together.	◯	◯	◯	◯	◯

Business Culture Design

The Culture Map—a preview

It turns out that the big issues hidden below the waterline are the decisive ones for corporate culture—although or even because they are so hard to see and grasp. They are what the visible consequences, the manifestations of corporate culture, are built on. They guide the behavior of people in organizations.

It thus soon became a crucial aspect of my work on corporate culture to make these important yet vague concepts tangible. I wanted to create a language that would describe the iceberg as a whole. As I consider myself a very visual person, I wanted this language to make a strong visual impression. Images have strong effects. Good representations are memorable. And what is on paper often has a greater impact.

These considerations led me to develop the Culture Map. During my research, I came across the work of the American psychologist Clare W. Graves and the many subsequent developments based on his theories. Isaac Newton supposedly said that he was able to see as far as he did only because he was standing on the shoulders of giants. The Culture Map, too, builds on the compelling ideas of great thinkers, which over the years I have consistently combined, supplemented, and adapted to the field of corporate culture. At the same time, I was fortunate in having the opportunity to work with a multitude of businesses and thus to encounter ever new organizational cultures. As a consultant, I have worked with well-known corporations and "hidden champions" as well as with small, family-owned enterprises. My interest in corporate culture took me from an Austrian industrial firm to an American consultancy, from working with Professor Malik in Switzerland to China, Japan, and Korea, and finally from Columbia University to a most enriching partnership and friendship with Science House in New York. All these experiences have influenced my approach to corporate culture. The Culture Map is the result of these professional and academic experiences. It is built on a scientific foundation, but comes truly alive in its practical application.

The Culture Map visualizes the iceberg; it explains the visible manifestations and shows to what foundations they can be traced. It will equip you with a language and vocabulary for what can usually be described only in the vaguest of terms. The Culture Map patterns will tell you if an over-long meeting is due to blue or green causes, or whether a high rate of fluctuation originates in orange or

Individualistic, dynamic values		Group-oriented, stabilizing values
	Purple cultures resemble tribes. They give their members a sense of security and identity. Members are loyal to their group, have trust in their own community and in its patriarchal leadership. Decisions are based on experience.	⬡
⬡	Tenacity, courage, and resolve are the main features of red cultures. Decisions are made quickly and followed by resolute action. Red cultures will let nothing stand in the way of implementation. There is no hesitation in discarding old ways. Internal conflicts are carried out openly.	
	Order, rules, and structures dominate blue cultures. They ensure reliability and continuity. People fulfill their tasks with a sense of duty and considerable endurance. Positions and responsibilities are assigned according to hierarchies.	⬡
⬡	An orientation towards performance is the hallmark of orange cultures. People strive for recognition of their personal achievements. They think tactically, are good at recognizing opportunity, and reach goals by pragmatic experimentation.	
	Green cultures foster a pleasant, friendly, harmonious atmosphere that puts people at the center. People have each other's well-being in mind and support each other. Decisions are made by common consensus; conflicts are avoided.	⬡
⬡	Yellow cultures are dominated by knowledge and curiosity. People love progress. They admire freedom of thought, critical discussions, and the opportunity to make new discoveries. Arguments follow logic and reason. Decisions are based knowledge of detail, data, and facts.	
	In aqua cultures, people follow a mission that makes the world a better place and creates meaning. People look beyond their own backyards and create open networks outside the confines of their own organizations. Decision-making is guided by pattern recognition and holistic systems thinking.	⬡

green factors. The Culture Map allows you to get to the root of the problem rather than trying to address only the symptoms.

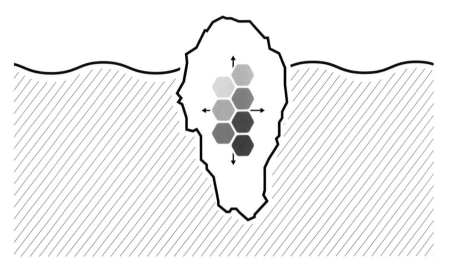

Each of the Culture Map's seven fields comprises certain characteristics of culture (or memes, see Chapter 2). The model's structure follows the logic of cultural evolution. With each step, from purple to aqua, cultures find increasingly complex solutions to the challenges facing them. At the same time, the Culture Map depicts the interplay between group-oriented, stabilizing values on the right and individualistic, dynamic values on the left.

But remember: The world of organizational cultures is a colorful one! No culture consists of one color alone. Every company, every department, every team contains elements of all seven colors.

Imagine the hexagons on the Culture Map as compartments in a toolbox: the red compartment contains red tools, the blue compartment blue tools etc. Your organization could use all tools from all compartments freely and equally often. Nonetheless, certain compartments are opened more frequently than others: If you've grown used to the red hammer, you're likely to keep reaching for it.

Organizations develop patterns of habit. In some organizations, conflicts may typically be avoided in a green way or pragmatically circumvented in an orange fashion, whereas in others they may be fought out in a red manner or resolved purple-style by the patriarch's ruling. When the chips are down, though all colors are available, habit forces recourse to learned patterns of behavior. Such patterns are formed by the differently-sized hexagons, which offer an insight into an organization's character. The following two examples illustrate this:

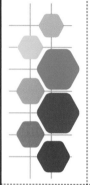

This organization is dominated by blue and green values, which suggests clear rules and structures in a harmonious working environment. The company is stable rather than dynamic, as the dominance of the right side of the Culture Map indicates.

The rate of fluctuation is low, and staff work thoroughly and reliably. Career paths are set well into the future—but promotions have more to do with time spent with the firm than with individual performance, let alone initiative. The organization's readiness to change is quite limited. Established structures and habits are firmly set and any disturbance by thinking outside the box or direct conflict is studiously avoided.

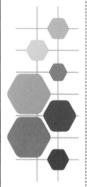

Orange ambition meets red fighting spirit: What matters to people here are personal success and individual advancement. They show initiative, refuse to be distracted from their objectives, and will not shy away from conflict—of which there is plenty.

This organization of individualists is held together primarily by a blue structure, which is supposed to offer a guiding framework for individual actions. This structure, however, is subject to dual pressure: First, rules tend to be stretched in the orange manner, and second, there is the red struggle against limitations of any kind.

Dynamic though this organization may be, it has a hard time focusing individual efforts towards the big picture, a common goal. The working atmosphere is dominated by friction, and human aspects are often sidelined.

Both cultural patterns undoubtedly have their strengths—but which can make a business truly successful today? A glance at the rise and fall of companies in the present provides the answers.

Chapter 2
Organizations as Organisms

The secret of viability

Walmart, the U.S. retail giant, and Sinopec, the Chinese natural gas and petroleum conglomerate, each employs over a million people. This places them among the largest specimens of a highly successful species: organizations.

Today's world is full of organizations. Very few people still work altogether by themselves. Hardly anything we come into daily contact with is not the product of an organization—or several. Even getting an apple from tree to shelf involves far more organizations than just the farmer and the supermarket: Businesses trading in seeds, fertilizer, and transport, for instance, and more often than not advertising agencies and packaging suppliers... It was not ever thus. The boom in formal organizations other than the institutions of the state began with the industrialization of the 19th century. Before, the work of farmers, artisans, and merchants was done largely by family members, perhaps with a few hired hands. The number, size, and interconnectedness of modern organizations as we know them today would have been quite unthinkable.

At first glance, today's powerful organizations look like a constant and stable presence. Appearances, however, deceive: In fact, the organizational landscape displays considerable coming and going. Like everything in life, individual organizations do not last forever. Since 1917, *Forbes* has been publishing an annual list of the largest American corporations. Eighty years later, the magazine reported that only 15 of the original top 100 were still in business.[4] A recent high-profile casualty was Kodak—an organization that seemed ubiquitous in my childhood.

Think back to earlier times: Where did you buy groceries, where clothing? What products did you use or consume regularly? If the businesses still exist, they are likely to have changed significantly over time. Consider Gebrüder Weiss, a logistics firm whose history can be traced back to the 14th century.[5] At the beginning stood messenger services around Lake Constance. Today, the company offers complex logistics solutions at 150 locations worldwide. It has remained viable over all these centuries and adapted to the new challenges posed by its environment, be they shipping on the lake, courier services across Alpine passes, or transporting goods to Shanghai.

Fit for their environment

Whereas some organizations vanish, others endure over generations. Nature has demonstrated the principle of viability for four billion years. The underlying principle is "the survival of the fittest." Unfortunately, this term has all too often been misunderstood as denoting the survival of the *strongest*. But nothing could be further from the truth: *fit*, as Darwin understood the term, means *fitting* into an ecological niche. Giganto-pithecus, a prehistoric ape some ten feet tall and weighing half a ton, went extinct 100,000 years ago. Whatever its problem was, it was not lack of strength. Other species of ape would most likely have come out on the short end of a direct confrontation. Nevertheless, they fit better to their environment, thus ensuring their survival. Jellyfish, too, have lived on earth for 500 million years. Yet far from being brawny, they consist mostly of water. Their strength lies in their organism's adaptedness to its environment.

Environment

Organism

Talk of the survival of the fittest should not mislead us into imagining evolution as a boxing match, a series of one-on-one contests. It is rather a continuous development with the end of maintaining viability amid complex, dynamic surroundings. In order to do so, organisms select ecological niches in which competition is minimized. If, for instance, all plants in a meadow

Business Culture Design

were to look for food in the same place, coexistence would be impossible. Their roots thus go to different depths. Following a comparable logic, businesses try to eliminate competition as far as possible by developing a unique selling point.

With reference to Darwin, the role of competition tends to be overemphasized. This comes at the expense of an important factor for survival: cooperation.

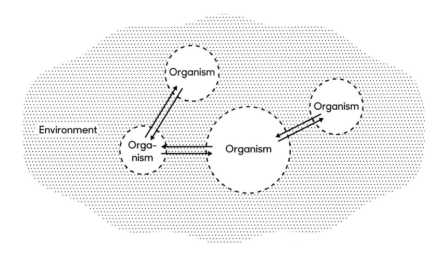

Modern evolutionary biology emphasizes the importance of symbiosis in nature: More than half of the earth's biomass exists in symbiotic relationships.[6] It is called co-evolution: life forms aim not to destroy one another, but to survive. By the same token, it would be hard to imagine modern organizations without cooperation. There can be barely a company that does not work together with others in some form or another. To get the world's largest airliner, the A380, off the ground, it took the contributions of about 1500 organizations from 30 countries.[7]

For both organisms in nature and organizations, the context in which to prove themselves is the dynamic environment.

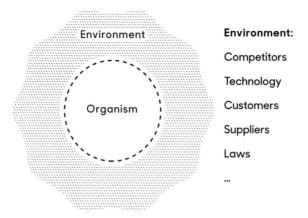

Environment

Environment:

Competitors

Technology

Customers

Suppliers

Laws

...

What aspects of a changing environment are truly relevant to a business must be determined in each specific case. For instance, not every organization is equally dependent on fluctuations in the price of oil. The expansion of the internet, too, had far more dramatic effects on newspapers and publishers than it did on hair salons. However, the example of the ride-sharing service Uber shows how some developments in today's networked world can reach across sectors. Traditional barriers to market entry are increasingly disappearing. Just a few years ago, taxi companies in Paris would hardly have imagined that an algorithm from California could threaten their business model.

To find the right fit in their environment is not, then, a one-off process for organizations. Adaptation is a non-stop task, and adaptability a basic condition. Lufthansa or McDonald's are not the same corporations they were even just a few years ago: The airline responded to the new realities of liberalized markets, online booking, and price-conscious consumers by reducing seat pitch and founding cheaper subsidiaries. For its part, the fast food chain has adapted too. It no longer just offers quick meals, but has added McCafés in which customers are invited to linger. Such changes affect not just the range of products offered, but also a company's self-understanding with regard to what it takes to succeed in a changing marketplace. As Jack Welch, a legend of leadership and long-time CEO of General Electric, once put it succinctly:

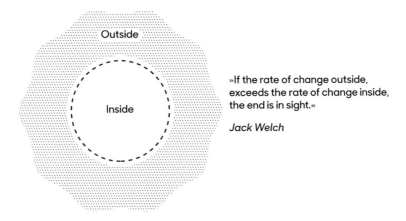

Outside

Inside

»If the rate of change outside,
exceeds the rate of change inside,
the end is in sight.«

Jack Welch

Besides adapting to environmental circumstances, there is another way for businesses to get fit: They can use innovation to influence their environment. Successful innovations change the organization's environment, or at least part of it. When Dietrich Mateschitz, the founder of Red Bull, started his energy drink business, he knew that there was no market for his product. But he was sure of one thing: that Red Bull would create its own market.[8] And that is what happened.

Starbucks, too, changed the environment in which it operated as a business. I remember my first visits to the United States at a time when it seemed almost impossible to get a decent cup of coffee. In the early 1990s, relatively few Americans felt the need to enjoy a cappuccino on their commute—yet now it has become a firm part of American culture. The company succeeded in influencing coffee-drinking habits in Europe, too, where most people long thought it an abomination to drink coffee from a paper cup with a plastic lid. Even in China, a country that was long considered a coffee-free zone, more and more coffee shops are popping up. That Starbucks now operates in such a coffee-friendly environment is no coincidence. It was created. Starbucks succeeded in molding an environment in which its business could succeed, that is, be viable.

Every new product or service has the potential to change customer behavior and thus a part of an organization's environment, no matter how small or large a business may be. Every organization can safeguard its survival by adapting or by changing its environment through innovation. In practice, however, it is hard to keep these two aspects apart. One never occurs altogether without the other, because innovations cause internal changes, and internal changes aim to improve the organization—that is how innovation works.

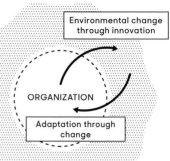

Managing complex systems

Ideas about how to keep organizations viable have changed considerably over time.

Imagine you were the boss of an early industrial organization, say around 1910. Your task is to organize production of a mechanical product, a gramophone for instance, with 100 barely trained workers. Maybe you are familiar with some of the ideas of Frederick Taylor that can help you run your factory. Or you may have heard about how one Henry Ford has begun to reimagine automobile production. Be that as it may, your goal is to optimize the production process in order to deliver quality goods at a competitive price. Your main focus is coordinating the workers in the manufacturing department, because that is where quality and efficiency decide on your ultimate success. The smoother production runs, the better the result will be. You do everything to ensure that your organization runs like a well-oiled machine. The first management ideas, which are emerging around this time, can help you— for instance the idea of dividing a complicated task into several simple steps on which the respective worker can then concentrate.

Now think ahead 50 years: The gramophone factory is gone, and the style of management has evolved. To coordinate workers on the production line efficiently and to ensure that they fulfill their assigned tasks correctly is no longer enough. The challenges have become more demanding, as have your workers. In your organization, leadership concepts are now in the ascendant that go far beyond the mere coordination of discrete tasks in the Taylorist manner. From your managers, too, you expect far more than just supervising processes. Managers are now supposed to assume the responsibility of leading people and the company as a whole to new heights.

Today, a further important developmental step can be discerned: Many businesses are experiencing that time-tested organizational concepts have reached their limits. Such concepts are not up to dealing with the complexity that has developed in and around organizations. Because the properties of complex systems are altogether different from those of complicated systems, let alone simple ones.

	Simple systems: the on/off switch. A simple system functions according to a limited number of monocausal if-then relationships. Relations between variables are not just easily recognized, but also stable and linear: A soft blow of the hammer will drive the nail into the wood only a bit, a harder blow will have a predictably stronger effect.
	Complicated systems: the mechanical clock. In complicated systems, too, clear linear relationships exist between cause and effect—but there are many more of them, for instance in the movement of a mechanical clock or watch with its many parts. That's what makes the matter complicated. A trained watchmaker will be able to discern how the parts hang together; the layman will find the matter quite difficult.
	Complex systems: an organism. Complex systems are to some degree opaque and incomprehensible. Their behavior cannot always be fully understood or predicted, for the individual components and the relationships between them change over time. An element's behavior has not one cause, but many. And these causes are themselves dynamic and mutually dependent. What is more, complex systems are open—they interact with their environment. Momentary glimpses give little indication of future development. For instance, it is impossible exactly to forecast the weather in two months' time, though thousands of stations deliver millions of individual readings of as many variables.

We might say: Something is complex when we can't figure it out completely, but when we also realize that its operation is not entirely random.[9] The behavior of workers, for instance, depends not on a single factor, but is influenced by a multitude of factors: factors within the organization may play a part, like rapport with the boss or the pay scale. Or perhaps an individual worker may be more influenced by a corporate mission statement she finds compelling or by a strong sense of loyalty to the company.

No doubt such individual factors are connected. And what happens outside organizations influences behaviors in the organization as well, from the overall economic climate to their private well-being.

Peter Drucker emphasizes how much the complexity of the challenges faced by organizations has grown. As one of the 20th century's foremost management thinkers, he described how, at the beginning of the 21st century, what had long held true was about to be overturned now, in the new millennium.[10]

Placing these aspects side by side shows that things used to follow a fairly orderly course. Competition took place within a sector. Each product had a specific application, and for every application there was a specific product: Clothing was made from wool, not synthetic fibers; capital was provided by the bank and not venture capitalists; telephones could be used only to make and receive calls. It was easy to identify in what sectors a company did business and who the competitors were. Workers were trained to perform the specific tasks for which the company had hired them. The expertise they acquired in the process was of relatively little value in other industries.

Yet now, the lines between markets and industries have become blurred. Stable categories have given way to open systems. There are barely any stable markets left on whose predictable demand companies might rely. Customers have taken control and are dictating new realities. Workers are no longer mere resources for production, but bring to a business the knowledge and abilities that define it.

Modern organizations can no longer be compared to well-oiled machines, but to complex, living organisms.

A business's success now depends to a far lesser extent than before on individuals at the top, in the words of Peter Senge, an organizational scientist at MIT and best-selling author: "It is no longer sufficient to have one person learning for the organization, a Ford or a Sloan or a Watson or a Gates. It's just not possible any longer to 'figure it out' from the top, and have everyone else following the orders of the 'grand strategist.'"[11]

Today, knowledge and abilities are the possession of a diversity of people within the organization. In situation upon situation, they are compelled to make the right decisions independently and autonomously, because it is no longer possible to determine in advance what needs to be done in every imaginable situation. For

Then	Now
The organization is the "master," the workers its "servants." The organization owns the means of production. Staff are dependent on the organization.	Knowledge is the primary means of production. Workers own knowledge and put it at the organization's disposal. Staff and organization are mutually dependent.
A majority of the workforce is with the organization for life, working full time, every day. Their salary is the foundation of their life.	People delivering services to an organization are decreasingly likely to do so for life. They work with organizations in flexible and temporary arrangements.
The most efficient way of producing a product is to combine as many of the relevant activities as possible under a single roof. For instance, Ford manufactured not only all parts for its cars, but also steel, glass, and tires. The company even owned rubber plantations in Brazil as well as the means of shipping rubber to its factories in the U.S.	Complete integration no longer makes sense. The knowledge required for each activity is highly specialized, while transaction costs have sunk greatly. Organizations collaborate in complex networks.
The market power of suppliers and producers is based on having information about products that customers neither have nor can access.	Customers have information or can obtain it. Power migrates to customers. Suppliers are not so much vendors as buyers on behalf of customers.
Each technology has its industry and each industry its technology.	Hardly any industry-specific technologies are left. Knowledge that can be used successfully in one industry can be applied to an altogether different industry.

situations may arise in which even established standards and the experience of years have no good advice to offer. This means that leaders and workers must act in the organization's interest without having exact and case-specific instructions to fall back on.

When Eric Schmidt took over as CEO of Google, his favorite question, "What's different now?", soon became the company's design plan. He found that not only technology had changed, but so had the balance of power: "Power has shifted from companies to consumers [...]. Meanwhile, within companies the power has shifted as well. Individuals and small teams can have a massive impact ."[12]

He set about creating a new company for new times by consciously designing an organization for "smart creatives," with a culture attractive to such people and an organization able to create functionality in a complex world, by means including fluent planning processes, open information systems, and transparent decision-making.

Increased complexity confronts businesses with a view not only to the demands of the market place, but also to their workforce. Modern organizations compete not just for customers, but also for the best workers—and they are more demanding than ever. A look at popular employer rankings shows that the most desirable companies are not necessarily those known for paying the highest salaries. People ask for more; they are exacting knowledge-workers who freely and autonomously choose to place their services at the organization's disposal. It is the best and brightest that choose companies that can offer them an attractive culture. Purpose, autonomy, and opportunities for personal development often mean more than pay in terms of motivation.[13] Integrity, sustainability, and work-life-balance may also be critical factors in choosing an employer today. In earlier times, virtually nobody in their right mind would have asked about the possibility of a sabbatical in their initial job interview.

Business Culture Design

Over the last few decades, the demands on organization design have changed especially with regard to two dimensions. Demands on an organization's functionality have increased, as have the demands of the people within the organization. Both call for conscious Business Culture Design.

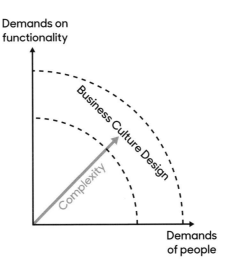

The essential abilities of a modern business are built on complexity. Only thus can organizations respond dynamically to the environment or change it. They can find new solutions and determine their own behavior. They just need to want to do it and go for it proactively—and that is where corporate culture comes in. Whereas the focus used to be on optimizing tasks and processes, and on leading people, the challenge now is to create an organizational culture that keeps the "organization organism" alive and well. Culture is responsible for an organization's perceptions, thoughts, feelings, and actions. More than ever, culture is what determines the functioning of an organization and also its ability to bring together the people that can advance the organization's success.

To attain functionality and reach out to people by means of excellent design is nothing new in product and graphic design. Steve Jobs was convinced that "design is not just what it looks like and feels like. Design is how it works."[14] Functionality was a crucial demand he made on design. That design should reach people's hearts is also a key concern in the work of my uncle, the graphic designer Stefan Sagmeister. It is not least to him that I owe this insight: Good design touches people. Business Culture Design, too, is intended to serve functionality—and people. To this end, a perspective is chosen that considers a business not as a mechanical entity, but as a living—indeed human—organism. Culture is this organism's heart, mind, and soul.

Business Culture Design means recognizing the patterns in an organization's culture and to develop them consciously:

- Making cultural patterns visible offers decisive insights into the system's functioning. Phenomena whose cases were previously obscure can now be explained: why a strategy is not fully implemented, why conflicts keep erupting in one department but not in another, what really drives innovation, and much more.
- Consciously developing an organization's cultural patterns makes possible the kind of management that is up to today's complex challenges. Even if a business is forced to act in a barely predictable world—whether it is to respond to future challenges in a structured blue or pragmatic orange manner can be determined today. What is more, awareness of cultural patterns helps in grasping a culture's strengths and using them purposefully: introducing new products at red speed, for instance.
- Business Culture Design can help an organization put certain cultural patterns into place when and where they are needed to support viability and success: You can plan at which stages of the innovation process yellow creativity, green consensus, or blue structure are most appropriate.
- Business Culture Design prevents questions of strategy, leadership, or organization from being treated in isolation, but embeds and brings them to life in the context of a corporate culture.

There is, of course, no such thing as a simple "design switch" that can be flipped on. Culture designers are not mechanics, but can be compared rather to landscape gardeners. Consciously molding a corporate culture is indeed quite similar to cultivating a landscape. The fact is that every garden will develop regardless of the gardener's intervention, for every garden has a life of its own. A landscape gardener cannot prescribe growth, but she can intervene deliberately to control or encourage certain developments, for instance by ensuring that light and water are available where needed, or by separating or merging certain flower beds or plants and thus controlling exchange between them. She can also prune and graft where appropriate, and keep the growth of weeds in check.

The goal of a good landscape gardener will be to develop the garden as a whole. She will have to concentrate on particular corners from time to time, but knows that her ultimate concern is for the landscape in its entirety. She is also aware that plants influence each other, for instance the way in which tall plants can deprive smaller ones of sunlight. External influences can also control developments, for wind, sun, and rain form a dynamic environment, as do birds, insects, and other animals. They can even introduce new plants to the garden that can affect its balance.

Make no mistake: Business Culture Design is no substitute for management or leadership. Its purpose is rather to help deploy concepts of management and leadership appropriately. For it is only in full awareness of cultural patterns that access points for the right ideas can be reliably identified.

The dynamic of organizational elements

Organizations do not form by accident. People organize with a purpose in mind. In every social organism, it is thus possible to identify the constitutive elements of purpose, people, and structure. Culture as the fourth element emerges wherever people interact.

For a simple example of how such an organization organism works, consider two children setting up a roadside stall from which to sell home-made lemonade on a summer's day. They do so because they are sure that passers-by will be eager for refreshment on a hot day—that is their little organization's purpose. The people running the business are the two children, and their actions follow a simple structure: To do as much as possible together and share the profits. Of course, the children will not have made a conscious effort to think about their lemonade business's corporate culture. Yet culture nonetheless emerges from their interaction. They exchange opinions, values, and convictions and in doing so learn from and about each other. Habits and conventions form, which characterize and safeguard the functioning of the lemonade stand. For instance, a culture of trust emerges, in that both children need to be able to trust one not to make off with the proceeds while the other leaves to stock up on lemons.

It's only a matter of time before the two young entrepreneurs equip their organization with some elements of management. Being smart kids, they come up with a strategy: The stall is positioned close to an intersection and the lemons are sourced from the cheapest retailer. What was previously a loose structure of cooperation now becomes a conscious organization: One child squeezes lemons and mixes the lemonade, the other sells it. Although the relationship between the children is not that of staff and superior, their behavior will be guided by certain elements of leadership: They lead each other and themselves, set targets and coordinate their work.

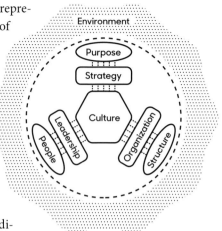

The analogy of the organism can be applied to any organization, be it a start-up, a small business, or a large corporation; be it a team, a department, or the entire company. The basic elements of the organization organism—people, purpose, and structure—are given in any organization. Culture emerges from them and determines how the organization as a whole perceives, thinks, feels, and acts—it is the mindset of the organism. The management elements—strategy, organization, and leadership—help guide the organization's fortunes. But these elements, too, are not simple levers by which to effect change. After all, there are no mono-causal relationships within the complex system of the organization-organism, where everything is connected to everything else. Strategy, leadership, and organization, too, exercise force on each other. And at the core of this construction stands culture, which exerts a decisive influence on all three dimensions.

Strategy for a purpose

It should require no explanation that a business strategy cannot be considered in disconnection from the business's purpose: The purpose indicates a general direction, and the strategy sketches the road that leads there. Whether or not the purpose is met depends critically on strategy. But the best strategy is of no use if the culture rejects it. For a developed strategy truly to come to life, it must be implemented, which is to say: anchored in the culture. Good strategy development always goes hand in hand with developing culture.

At the same time, the existing corporate culture affects work on strategy. In strongly yellow cultures, for instance, the work of strategy is based mainly on analyses and concepts. In purple cultures, on the other hand, strategy tends to be determined by the patriarch's gut feeling. Strongly aqua cultures think openly and with the long term in mind, whereas orange strategies are pragmatic and goal-oriented. An awareness of your own culture will help you design a strategic process that is coherent in content and culturally effective.

What purpose is to be pursued also depends on culture. Some cultures are quick to reorient themselves, others are rigid in pursuit of a traditional goal, though the market may no longer demand it. This relationship, too, is reciprocal: Culture not only influences the purpose— the purpose, in turn, exerts a strong pull on culture.

Leading people

A similar level of complexity characterizes the interplay of people, leadership, and culture: People leave their mark on culture, and culture leaves its mark on people. It stands to reason that a culture depends on who is part of it in the first place. After all, that's why recruitment and personnel decisions are so important in developing a culture.

Leaders are particularly important shapers of culture. How to behave at work is not something that staff learn from a glossy booklet, but from the everyday conduct of their leaders. They, to their staff, are examples of what is considered "desirable behavior" inside the company, and are imitated consciously or otherwise (more on this in Chapter 2). For instance, staff are unlikely to adhere to strict blue rules for meetings if their leaders express their yellow/orange free-spiritedness by regularly turning up late.

Furthermore, culture determines what kind of people are attracted and hired by a company, and who rises to the top. Sometimes a company will think that filling a key position with a star player brought in from outside can provide a simple way of effecting a strategic reorientation and solving its cultural problems. But usually that isn't enough. For instance, I know of companies that recruited staff from Google to develop their online store or placed someone from Apple at the head of their marketing department. In both cases, the "stars" soon left in despair, for neither they nor their ideas were accepted by the organization-organism. Their expertise may have been impeccable, but they were no match for the dominant corporate culture—in turn confirming staff in their view that "outsiders just don't fit in."

However, leadership's influence on culture is not limited to executives, but extends to all leadership systems that control behavior: Systems of pay, time-logging and controlling, performance reports, career prospects, etc. All these leave their mark on culture while being its product in turn.

The organization of structure

Order parameters for the organization of structure cover the spectrum from job listings and working hours to the large questions of organization, like the structuring of business activities across sectors, assigning responsibilities, or general mechanisms of coordination. Formally defined structures and procedures give direction to individual behavior. Even supposed questions of detail, like whether people work in open-plan offices or alone behind closed doors, do much to shape culture.

Agreements on how a business wishes to organize itself can both limit and promote the functioning of the organization-organism: If core time with mandatory attendance is set from Monday to Thursday, 10 a.m. to 4.30 p.m., then the likelihood of finding people in their offices during that time is greatly increased. This adds reliability and predictability, and strengthens the group-oriented right-hand side of the Culture Map. The limitations are equally clear: Staff can work from home only on Fridays, to the possible annoyance for the freedom-loving left-hand side of the map.

I already mentioned that culture eats strategy for breakfast. One might add: "… and structure for lunch!" Culture decides how structure is lived. Like changes of strategy, reorganizations do not become reality just because they are set down in writing. They become reality only once they have taken root in culture.

Business Culture Design

Assumptions in the deeps

Remember the iceberg model from chapter 1? The elements of the organization-organism can be arranged within it, too: Above the surface, you can see the organization's visible manifestations, i.e. purpose, structure, and people.

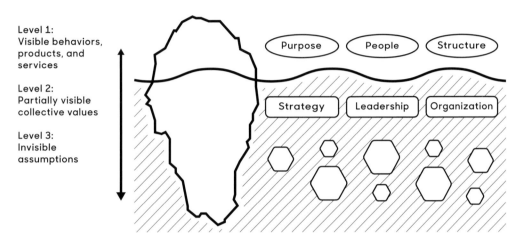

Level 1:
Visible behaviors, products, and services

Level 2:
Partially visible collective values

Level 3:
Invisible assumptions

Purpose People Structure

Strategy Leadership Organization

Appearing a little blurred beneath the surface are collective agreements on operating the business. In the deeps lurk culture's invisible assumptions and attitudes. Edgar Schein, a trailblazing thinker on corporate culture, has described these three levels of culture, and how the invisible assumptions influence the upper levels.[15] If one is to create an effect above the surface, it is sometimes necessary to dive deep to find and treat not just symptoms, but actual causes.

This was also the opinion of legendary CEO Lou Gerstner. Gerstner took the helm of IBM in the early 1990s, when this dinosaur of the IT world was threatened by extinction. The era of the mainframe computer was over, and with it the company's foundation. Many experts thought breaking up the huge conglomerate into its component parts was the only plausible solution. That way, they argued, at least parts of the corporation could survive. But Lou Gerstner had different ideas. He set about rebuilding the venerable, long successful, but now somewhat unwieldy giant. The changes he made were fundamental and painful. New strategies were developed, structured, altered, and staff replaced.

All these measures were taken with one aim in mind: to change corporate culture. Many years after the successful turnaround, Lou Gerstner wrote a book called *Who Says Elephants Can't Dance?*, in which he recalls: " I came to see, in my time at IBM, that culture isn't just one aspect of the game—it is the game!"[16]

Culture is at the center of the organization-organism, in connection and exchange with all the other functional elements. Culture thus affects all your company's workings: every sphere, every department, even every team. Culture has the power to reach into every section of a business. Neglecting it can have consequences in the most disparate places.

It is not a matter of chance which culture stands at an organism's center. But only by knowing what culture is and how it develops can you shape it proactively.

Culture as a competitive advantage for humanity

An objective, scientific gaze at the human genome may somewhat deflate human pride: Humans share more genetic information with two species of chimpanzee than those chimpanzees do with other apes.[17] The good news is that science also confirms that we, as human beings, are in certain respects unique and clearly set apart from the remainder of the animal kingdom. As Richard Dawkins, the famous evolutionary biologist at the University of Oxford, has put it: "Are there any good reasons for supposing our own species to be unique? I believe the answer is yes. Most of what is unusual about man can be summed up in one word: 'culture.'"[18]

Admittedly, compared with other creatures, human beings are neither particularly strong nor fast. We can't fly or last long underwater. Unlike our cats, we are likely to break our bones when falling down the stairs. But: We invented stairs and domesticated the cat! The competitive disadvantages we face against other species are compensated many times over by our ability to find creative solutions to problems. Steve Jobs was fascinated by this human ability. As he once told an interviewer:[19]

I read an article when I was very young in Scientific American. *It measured the efficiency of locomotion for various species on the planet. For bears, chimpanzees, raccoons, and birds, and fish, … How many kilocalories per kilometer do they spend to move? And humans were measured too. The condor won! It was the most efficient. Mankind, the crown of creation came in with a rather unimpressive showing about a third way down the list. But somebody had the brilliance to test a human riding a bicycle. It blew away the condor, all away off the charts! […] Humans are tool builders. We build tools that can dramatically amplify our innate human abilities.*

The ability to develop a bicycle nicely illustrates our species' true strength. We may not be the strongest, biggest, or fastest—but we are remarkably good problem-solvers.

Generally speaking, it is possible to distinguish four levels on which creatures solve problems.[20] The first two—problem-solving based on genes and memory—are widespread throughout the animal kingdom. But the third and the fourth—forming hypotheses and developing solutions—are exceedingly rare, and, where they do occur, tend to be rudimentary in comparison to human abilities.

As soon as a human has solved a problem, the solution is not available to her alone, but becomes part of human development. Others can build ideas of their own on this solution.

When we consider that human culture has, for hundreds of thousands of years, enabled a development where one idea leads to the next and each solution is the foundation for anther, it soon becomes apparent just how different we are from other creatures. They may be bigger or stronger, but nature has endowed us with the bigger and stronger brain—a brain that makes culture possible.

Level	Source	
1	Genes	**Solutions are innate.** What do you do to keep your eyes' sensitive cornea clean and lubricated? You blink—around 25 times per minute, without ever having to think about it. Each time you do so, your eyelid spreads teardrops across the eye's surface. Evolution has built a solution to the problem of dry eyes firmly into your nervous system.
2	Memory	**Solutions are based on experience.** Anyone who once burned their fingers on a hot cookie tray will long remember the pain. Our memory records experiences and uses them as yardsticks for future behavior. In other words, we learn from experience.
3	Reason	**Solutions are based on hypotheses.** There's no need to try out everything. The hypothesis that the hot cookie tray might burn our fingers can keep us from hurting ourselves in the first place. And thinking through the situation critically can lead us to various possible solutions. We might, for instance, grab a mitten from our winter wardrobe and thus invent the oven mitt. A new solution, courtesy of reason.
4	Culture	**Solutions are based on solutions.** How to do you know how to tie your shoelaces? Most likely it wasn't your idea. Nor was the oven mitt, the use of which you probably copied from your parents. The larger part of things that make life easier is based on solutions that others have come up with before us. As human beings, we benefit from the considerable advantage of being able to draw on solutions developed by other people for our own solutions—no matter if we ask them, watch them, read about it, or are told by third parties. Our behavior is thus founded on experiences that we did not have to make ourselves. We can exchange thoughts and combine them freely. And that's what we do.

Biology and culture

Each human being is part biology, part culture. Whereas our biology is based on a fixed set of genes, our culture is built on units that are not fixed, but highly dynamic. These cultural units are called "memes."

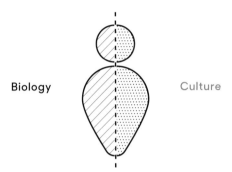

The term "meme" (plural "memes") was popularized in the 1970s by Richard Dawkins in his book *The Selfish Gene*. Genes alone did not seem sufficient to him to explain the evolution of human beings. While "gene" was the accepted term for the replicator in the process of biological evolution, he was missing a term for the counterpart in biological evolution. He thus abbreviated the Greek word *mimeme*, which means "to imitate," to "meme," which happens to sound a bit like gene, producing a neat symmetry of biological genes and cultural memes.[21]

Genes are the units of information that determine an organism's flesh and blood; whereas memes are the units that determine what ideas an organism carries. In a sense, memes are to our behavior as genes are to our body.[22] If you prefer to think in terms of IT, the concepts of "hardware" and "software" may provide an analogy: Genes are the patterns in our DNA that determine our hardware, like the color of our hair, blood group, height etc. Memes are the software code that programs our mind.

Every person is determined partly by genes, partly by memes. It is thus no great surprise that siblings who grow up together with their parents should display some similarities in their behavior. The reason is that besides their biological inheritance, there is a cultural inheritance that connects them.

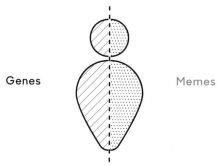

Genes   Memes

Imagine a baby whose biological parents are both Japanese. Immediately after its birth, this baby is taken to France, where it grows up in a French family (this thought experiments works just as well with Chinese babies in Brazil, American babies in Germany, or in any other combination). The Japanese baby learns French as its mother tongue, goes to school in a French village, makes French friends … in brief, this child will grow up with the ideas and habits of its surrounding culture and behave accordingly. Its genes will always suggest that its origins lie not in Europe but in Asia, yet its genes form only part of its identity. It will share many opinions and customs with the people in its surroundings, and not necessarily with those whose genes it has inherited.

Contagion through memes

Replication, variation, and selection are the ingredients that set off the algorithm of biological evolution, yet they also occur in the process of cultural evolution. Let me illustrate this point with a joke:

> *An entrepreneur meets a consultant.*
> *The entrepreneur asks: "If I ask you three questions, what will that cost me?"*
> *The consultant replies drily: "100,000 dollars."*
> *The entrepreneur: "Are you serious?"*
> *To which the consultant replies: "Yes. Now what's your third question?"*

If you find this joke amusing, you may contribute to its replication by telling it to someone else. But you might just tell it a little bit differently, for example by replacing the consultant with a lawyer. Or you might put the sum of $200,000 in place of $100,000 as the price for the three questions. Both would be variations of the original meme. What emerges is a copy of the joke, but not a precise one.

But perhaps you don't even enjoy telling jokes. In that case, the meme will not be able to multiply via you. Evolutionarily speaking, you do not contribute to its replication. Or you just happen to think that the joke is not very good and prefer to tell your friends another one. From all the jokes you know, you make the selection which ones to tell others.

Memes lodge themselves in our brains, always ready to infect others. Some of them are extremely successful: The idea of the "family" has spread across the world and it has existed, in numerous variations, for many thousands of years. Religions, too, are memes that have been able to spread across continents and centuries. Other memes are rather less successful. For instance, in Austria in the 1970s, an "Association of the Vertically Buried" was founded, which wanted to seal the dead in airtight plastic tubes and bury them upright. The idea found few adherents and the meme disappeared without a trace.

Great ideas consist of many small ideas. If your great idea is to cross the Atlantic in a boat you built yourself, then that is a meme. This meme might spread and deposit a copy in my brain. When infected, I will soon set about building a boat and hope to set sail before very long. The success or failure of your idea for sailing the Atlantic rests on many smaller ideas that decide the success or failure of your adventure. For instance, the way you build the hull or the shape of the sails each is a meme in its own right. To follow your main idea of sailing the Atlantic in a homemade boat, I may adopt some of these sub-ideas, but don't have to use them all.

A practical way of defining the unit of a meme is that it must be possible to imagine the meme in isolation. Crossing the Atlantic is a discrete unit, as are the mast or the boat's hull. These units can be transmitted to another brain alone or in combination with others.

Customer orientation is also a meme composed of many small units: How the phone is answered, for instance. Or whether the lights go out as closing time approaches, even though a customer is looming on the horizon. Or the manner of talking about customers in their absence. All this are discrete memes which, taken together, form the great meme of "customer orientation."

The transmission of memes

Memes can be transmitted back and forth, indeed, in all directions. Whereas genes are passed along vertically down the line of descent,[23] a far more dynamic picture emerges when we look at memes.

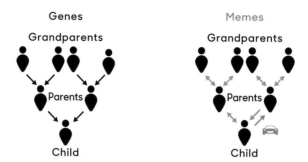

Memes are transmitted by imitation, for which children provide the most familiar examples. When my niece was a year old, she would hold anything that looked even remotely like a mobile phone to her ear. There is no way for such behavior to be encoded in her genes—not least because she is the first generation in her family tree to grow up with such devices. She exhibited such behavior because she had observed it in others and imitated it. The "cellphone memes" had successfully infected her. However, imitation is a process that is restricted neither to youth nor to top-down relationships, but can take place in all directions. When a young man buys a sports car and his father, finding youth to be wasted on the young, follows suit by buying a similar car, we may observe the bottom-up transmission of memes. What is more, transmission of memes is far from being restricted to the vertical. Memes are constantly being transmitted horizontally, too: between siblings, among friends, by television and so forth. What we see is a complex web of meme channels, with transmission taking place in multiple dimensions.

Some memes we adopt unwittingly: that tune we just can't get out of our heads, for example. Others we imitate consciously, for instance when we study the behavior of a colleague who just received a desirable promotion.

Business Culture Design

Yet what memes we encounter is far from coincidental. Not only parents spend much time and effort trying to instill certain values and manners in their children. Businesses, too, are far from uninterested in what mindsets drive their organization. They decide where blue memes foster reliability, where red memes encourage risk-taking, or where yellow memes are curious for new ideas.

We are particularly aware of the memes that are established in an organization when we start a new job. The dress code is only the start. As a new hire, one is likely to start on the new job with a pre-existing set of memes and thus to dress as one is accustomed to. We may than notice the raised eyebrows of our new colleagues, for whom we are dressed too formally or too casually. And that is just one of the more obvious adjustments we might have to make. There are many areas of working life to which we tend to bring preconceived notions, formed from experience: what kind of hierarchy is in place, how meetings are conducted, when to send an e-mail or when to pick up the phone instead, when to break for lunch, and so on. The set of memes one has personally labored to cultivate collides more or less gently with the atmosphere created by the other meme sets in the new office.

This new working climate, an as yet unknown corporate culture, may at first feel unfamiliar, in some aspects irritating – and the feeling is likely to be mutual. As a rule, however, time takes care of such differences. Memes are exchanged and replaced, consciously or otherwise. This exchange is by no means a one-way street: The new arrival's memes are just as keen to spread. They may face an uphill battle against the massed forces of set ways, but then, people are often put into certain positions in order to spread their thoughts and ideas. Or, to put it another way: To infect their colleagues with their memes.

Healthy, successful, and obstinate memes

My former boss, Professor Fredmund Malik, used the phrase "mind pollution" when he came across a poor understanding of management in a company, and considered it one of the principal causes of management errors.[24] And indeed it is hard for individual leaders to break through ingrained patterns of thought and behavior once bad practices have spread throughout an organization.

When Lou Gerstner set about rebuilding IBM, at the time something of a corporate dinosaur, he identified two principal factors that characterized IBM's culture.[25] They were responsible for encouraging the spread of particular memes and systematically keeping away others. One factor was the IT giant's sustained and overwhelming success. Lacking real competition and enjoying healthy profit margins and dominant market positions, the company gradually lost sight of external realities. The forces of a highly competitive marketplace, which inevitably produce certain memes in a company, were absent—it was far preferable to deal with more agreeable matters. The second factor, too, served to keep out or block certain memes: a looming antitrust action hung over IBM like the sword of Damocles. Gerstner recalls how words like "market share" or "competition" were systematically expunged from written communications and internal meetings. Phrases such as "beating the competition" or "prevailing in the marketplace" were taboo. But if staff are banned from talking about measuring up to competitors, let alone gaining market share, it is going to lead to certain habits of mind.

Pioneers of meme theory, like Richard Dawkins, Susan Blackmore, or Daniel Dennett, argue that memes are self-guided, indeed, are capable of acting self-interestedly. Memes, in other words, are indifferent to their host's well-being. All they care about is to stay alive by self-replication, in much the way that a virus spreads without having the interests of its hosts at heart. To put it more kindly: Ideas have lives independent of their creators. They can infect others and thus continue to develop and spread, outliving their creator. In evaluating memes, we thus would be well advised to distinguish between memes that are successful (from the meme's perspective) and healthy (i.e. beneficial to their hosts). Whether a meme is successful or not is a fairly easy question to answer. The point to consider is whether or not it succeeds in crossing over to and establishing itself in other minds. Far more difficult is deciding whether a meme is healthy or unhealthy.

For instance, an overwhelming majority of humanity now agrees that doing away with slavery was a good thing, a healthy meme. And it is, moreover, a successful meme, having spread far and wide. Ecological awareness, too, is a healthy meme—albeit one that still struggles to establish itself in many minds. Other memes are generally considered unhealthy, in spite of their considerable success.

That smoking is cool is an unhealthy meme, but quite a successful one. And some supposedly healthy memes may only later reveal themselves to be unhealthy, for instance one that leads its host to join a religious cult.

Some memes bring both advantages and disadvantages to their hosts. A couple of beers after work with your colleagues on a Friday night may not be positively good for your health, but is apt to improve everybody's mood and thus contribute to mental health. What is more, relationships cultivated and information gleaned in the process may turn out to be useful. This meme is both healthy and unhealthy; it has spread with great success in London, for instance—rather less so in Tehran.

Other memes are good for the infected person, but less so for others who are left to deal with the consequences: Things that may advance individual careers need not benefit the organization as a whole.

And then there are memes that are highly successful, but really make very little difference, for better or for worse. Guests enter hotel bathrooms around the world to find the first leaf of the toilet roll folded into a neat triangle. The idea spread quickly and widely, but is of little import.

Whether one judges a meme to be healthy or unhealthy also depends in part on what memes one happens to be infected with oneself. A purple culture tends to see yellow individualism as a danger to the group's cohesion. Yellow cultures, on the other hand, will contend that it is the purple tendency to groupthink that is dangerous.

A glance at human history reveals that, countless setbacks notwithstanding, healthy memes have triumphed again and again, influencing the development of our species for the better. After hundreds of thousands of years of evolution and considerable experience in a variety of cultural settings, our brains have become quite adept at selecting those memes that seem the most advantageous to us. Consequently, the philosopher Daniel Dennett has argued that "we have good reason to believe that our meme-immunological systems are not hopeless—even if they are not foolproof."[26] No doubt stupid ideas will always be with us. But we need not despair, for it is in our power to decide what ideas ultimately prevail. That memes have lives of their own does not absolve us from the responsibility of deciding what ideas to think up, adopt, preserve, and develop.[27] We help memes to spread.

High-speed evolution

Biologically speaking, humankind has not changed much over the last few millennia. Even comparing a caveman to his modern counterpart, we must admit that there are barely any anatomical differences: Like us, our ancestors had long legs allowing them to walk upright, hands with which to grasp objects, and a large skull with room for powerful eyes and much else. Nonetheless, they seem to have little in common with us: Their clothing and hair would strike us a rather unusual, as would, if we could hear them, their language. Their social mores would most likely seem wildly unfamiliar. So whereas hardly anything has changed about the biological setting, a great deal has happened culturally.

In fact, culture changes so quickly that we can observe cultural evolution taking place before our own eyes. Within our own lifetimes we see cultures come and go. You may remember your haircut in the 1980s—well, it seemed like a good idea at the time… Looking at the exchange of memes across the sweep of human history, certain innovations catch the eye—certain memes—which in turn have exponentially accelerated the exchange of memes.

- *Speech*: Undoubtedly a milestone in cultural development. What a meme booster! By means of speech, humans are able to exchange ideas and information.
- *Writing*: Useful though speech may be, even the loudest utterance soon fades away. What luck, then, that humankind invented writing. By means of graphic symbols, information can be transmitted independently of personal contact, through cave paintings as well as books.
- *Mobility*: Over the last few centuries, the personal exchange of memes has received a considerable boost. People travel from one corner of the world to the other, scattering memes along the way. And we don't even have to go as far as the monuments erected by conquerors—pizza and kebabs can also serve as tasty examples.
- *Internet*: Digitalization and interconnectedness have taken the exchange of information to a new level. In the internet age, memes travel the world at incredible speeds.[28] A single meme can now reach more people than ever before.

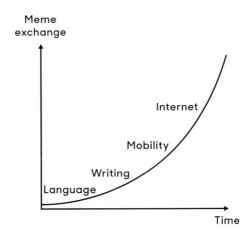

Which memes predominate in your organization, how healthy or unhealthy they are, and which ones should be encouraged for future benefit, can be controlled by conscious Business Culture Design. The process reveals the extent to which memes shape perception and thus influence behavior within your organization.

Collective constructivism

We like to believe that we see the world the way it is. But in fact, we see the world the way we are. Ultimately, we reduce information and use it to construct our own image of the world, our personal view of things.

Our senses are continually exposed to a tremendous onslaught of information. Research has shown that every second, information equivalent to one billion bits meets our sensory organs.[29] What is essential to processing this information is not so much to record it in full, but rather reducing it. Hence, our brain cuts the incoming data down by a factor of one million, to about 100 bits per second. Thus filtered, incoming information is stripped of irrelevant ballast. This reduced amount of data is subsequently combined with previously stored information and enriched, to approximately 10 million bits per second.

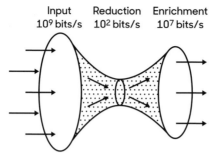

Input   Reduction   Enrichment
10^9 bits/s 10^2 bits/s 10^7 bits/s

This function allows us to grasp situations in their entirety by only a few ordering parameters. We are thus able to reach important decisions quickly and react accordingly: For a caveman, for example, it was enough just to hear a wildcat's hiss to draw the appropriate conclusions. For the knowledge that the hiss would likely be followed by the animal itself was already saved.

This "bottleneck of perception" not only reduces and enriches information; above all, it personalizes it. Reality is thus dependent on personal perception; it is the brain's interpretation. The brain constructs all we know abut reality.

Many great thinkers have addressed this process by which reality is constructed. Already the natural philosophers of the pre-Socratic era puzzled over how constructed reality might reflect actual reality. Since the end of last century, at the latest, when the studies of Paul Watzlawick, Heinz von Foerster, or Ernst von Glaserfeld became established under the heading of constructivism, their core idea has gained wide acceptance: What we perceive as reality is personally constructed.

Our memes influence which parts of information are selected to be perceived and absorbed, and which fall victim to reduction. And above all, they decide what the information we absorb means for us personally. This is well expressed by the joke in which a proud mother, observing the passing parade, exclaims: "Just look! Except for my Johnny, they're all marching out of step!"[30] Banksy, the graffiti artist, also understood how the interpretation of perception falls back onto the perceiver when he sprayed the following insight onto a truck: "The grumpier you are, the more assholes you meet…"[31] Anyone infected with ill-tempered memes is all the more likely to construct reality accordingly.

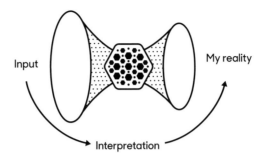

Input   My reality

Interpretation

Our own surroundings and the people in them help both to filter information and interpret it. "At any given moment, reality is what we perceive and what most of those perceiving it have agreed on," explains Professor Singer of the Max Planck Institute for Brain Research.[32] Hence, some researchers go so far as to speak of "the social construction of reality."[33]

The process of constructing social reality begins with habituation: Actions that have proved useful are repeated and thus become a habit. This saves a considerable amount of mental resources. We could not exist if we had to reconsider each and every action each time we perform it. When other people adopt these actions, they become institutionalized, and the relevant memes spread. Such a socially institutionalized reality is the foundation of any social order. It gives people routine and security, and endows social life with a degree of reliability. What we define as "normal" tends to reflect that reality. A continental European, for instance, who disembarks from the car ferry or train in England, will soon find what hard work it is to leave behind socially formed habits even for a moment. The knowledge that Britain drives on the left does not suffice to provide immunity against lapsing into accustomed, habitual behavior. Habituation of the kind that shapes society is also important in business. Whether the task is filing taxes, opening a branch office, or setting up a new production facility—undertakings that may be difficult and time-consuming the first time around will seem less so the second time, and sooner or later they become routine. The more a narrow track is travelled, the more it becomes an established road. Experience, as it were, leaves traces in the brain, as it does in corporate culture.

But constantly following the same beaten track means missing out on new experiences. Sooner or later, the track becomes a deep ditch, in which it is impossible to see anything to the left or right. Then, there is only one way to go: that carved out by past experience. The danger this results in for businesses becomes particularly apparent in times of change, when the companies that thrive are surprisingly often the seemingly less experienced ones: Nobody knew more about video rental than Blockbuster—until Amazon and Netflix came along and took over. In an infamous interview given just after the first iPhone was presented,[34] Microsoft's then CEO Steve Ballmer poured scorn on the new kid on the block. The all-important business customer, he said, would never accept a phone without a keypad. And what was more, Microsoft already sold millions of cellphones a year, whereas Apple had not yet sold a single one.

Mutual confirmation of reality

When people interact, they exchange realities with each other. They infect each other with their memes. The more people are infected with a reality, the more real it seems. A society's members mutually confirm each other's interpretation of reality and thus confirm their shared worldview.

The study *They Saw a Game* is considered a classic piece of research on collective perception. In 1954, it examined how an audience composed of students at Princeton and Dartmouth perceived a football game between the two college teams.[35] Whether they had followed it live or watched a recording of it later, it was as if the students had seen two different games. A particularly polarizing question was which team had started to play gratuitously rough. Dartmouth students interpreted their perception in a manner entirely different from their peers at Princeton. Two different realities collided.

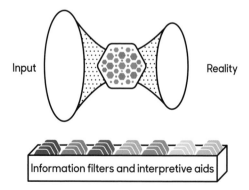

The seven colors of the Culture Map also represent seven different perspectives; seven filters, as it were, through which he world is perceived, and seven ways subsequently to interpret what has been perceived. A reality strongly constructed by a green culture will counsel generosity and leniency in a case where the blue reality finds it quite natural to enforce the rules, and the aqua reality considers and balances the overarching interest of the whole. Such cultural patterns find their own truth and act accordingly.

Chapter 3
The Culture Map

Features of the Culture Map

The Culture Map is a model for interpreting evolutionary memes in the context of corporate culture. Models are simplified depictions of a reality: They reduce a complex set of variables to something comprehensible, tangible, and testable. Albert Einstein once said that things ought to be made as simple as possible, but no simpler than that. The Culture Map adheres to that principle: It is easy to learn and apply. It gives a vivid representation of cultural patterns and makes them easy to describe. At the same time, it makes no claim to explain every conceivable situation to the level of its minutiae. What the Culture Map does is to bring order to the sometimes confusing world of memes.

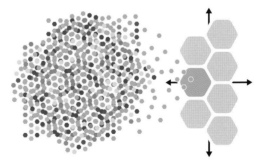

The model represents the traits of a culture as seven colored hexagons. Each hexagon is a cluster for particular memes. Since each of these meme groups is assigned to a color, it is possible to refer to red memes, blue memes, etc.

Visualizing culture

Visual representation is a key feature of the Culture Map. At first sight, seven hexagons are discernible, each of a different color. The relative sizes of the colored areas indicate the strength of the corresponding memes in a particular culture.

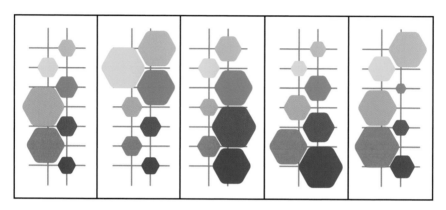

The seven hexagons of the Culture Map broadly follow the "levels of human existence" as defined by the psychologist Clare W. Graves (1914–1986).[36] Graves identified various value systems that influence perception, thinking, feeling, and behavior. His theory was an attempt at explaining why people do what they do. Although his work predates the idea of memes, Graves was sure that on the one hand, people create culture, but that, conversely, culture also leaves its stamp on people. Graves's research differs fundamentally from other contemporary theories. He did not believe in an ultimate state of development that could be attained by people or cultures.

Graves left to posterity not a definitive doctrine, but a collection of impressive ideas spread across manuscripts, articles, lectures, and notes.[37] They were collected by his colleagues and subsequently developed and reinterpreted in many ways by various writers, thinkers, and practitioners. The best-known among these efforts are probably the works of Christopher Cowan and Don Edward Beck, which in turn gave rise to further elaborations. Among other things, their book *Spiral Dynamics* represents the first attempt to color-code Graves's "levels."[38] Graves also served the philosopher Ken Wilber as orientation in developing his Integral Theory[39] of mind and consciousness; Said Elias Dawalabani used the framework for his macroeconomic studies;[40] and Marion Küstenmacher et al. to describe religious spirituality.[41] In the context of organizations, Frederic Laloux, in his *Reinventing Organizations*, reminded a wider audience of Graves's achievements. Graves's friend and colleague Christopher Cowan once remarked that "Graves urges his readers to rise above established disciplinary boundaries […] and to examine culture, adult behavior, thinking, motivation, management and learning from many points of view, each of which can hold elements of truth."[42]

In this sense, the interpretation of Graves's research regarding modern organizations is an element of the Culture Map—one of several, however. The descriptions of the individual hexagons, like the overall logic of the Culture Map, combine Graves's legacy with insights gained in disciplines such as biology, psychology, and anthropology. Furthermore, these descriptions incorporate the results of leadership and organizational studies, and particularly the real-life experience of working with people in businesses worldwide, ranging from globally operating Fortune 500 companies via family-owned businesses to non-profit organizations.

In spite of its evolutionary component, the Culture Map is not a typical model of the kind that describes the course of a company's successful development as a sequence of phases or stages. Instead, the model explains how the traits of different value systems influence a company's success in the modern world of business. The values that end up "highest" on the ladder are not always the ones that promise the most success.

The y-axis: the evolutionary path

Besides the hexagons' colors, their positioning along the two axes of the Culture Map is significant. The hexagons' size changes according to the culture, their positioning does not. It follows a system of its own, in which the y-axis traces the "evolutionary path" these memes take.

Whether or not cultural evolution follows a particular path is a question to which anthropologists across the centuries have given very different answers. For a long time, even experts had a hard time making sense of newly discovered cultures and situating them in their idea of the world: In the Middle Ages, scholars like Thomas Aquinas referred to alien cultures as "natural slaves." And even in the 19th century, leading cultural anthropologists like Lewis Henry Morgan regarded foreign cultures as "savages," who were still at the beginning of a linear process of evolution that would have them pass through "barbarism" before developing into "civilized men." It took till the early 20th century for the insight to take hold that matters were rather more complicated, and that cultural development does not proceed up a scale of pre-defined, hierarchically ordered levels in order to culminate in a supposedly perfect—or at least the best—state.[43]

What the history of humankind instead reveals is a pattern of development towards increasing complexity. From Stone Age hunter-gatherers to the globally interconnected societies of today, cultural development follows a path that, admittedly, is somewhat ill-defined and more often than not a bit rocky. The sociologist Robert Wright analyzes this path of social development in his bestselling book *Nonzero*:

When you look beneath the roiled surface of human events, beyond the comings and goings of particular regimes, beyond the lives and deaths of the "great men" who have strutted on the stage of history, you see an arrow pointing tens of thousands of years ago and continuing to the present. And, looking ahead, you see where it is pointing. [...] Interdependence expands, and social complexity grows in scope and depth.[44]

Over time, then, humankind developed ever more complex solutions to its many challenges—setting itself ever more complex challenges in the process. The tools brought to light by archaeologists display the essence of this development. As a rule of thumb, it holds true that the deeper you dig, the more simple the objects you find are likely to be. Throughout history, existing tools were replaced by more sophisticated new inventions. Nowadays, bows and arrows are the hunting instruments of choice only for nostalgics. Yet other objects have hardly changed at all over the course of millennia: A modern hammer is essentially the same tool that you would find in a museum, and the wheel is such an excellent invention that its proverbial reinvention truly is unnecessary.

A similar pattern applies to the development of societies: Some cultural elements have changed over time, yet others have not. The people of today are plagued by worries largely unknown to their ancestors: Will I get the promotion? Am I going to miss my flight? Why on earth does my son want a cartilage piercing? Yet other concerns seem timeless—lovesickness, for example. And then there are worries that once seemed terrifying, but over which few people today are likely to lose much sleep: that the gods might withhold much-needed rainfall on account of inadequate sacrifices, perhaps. Values develop accordingly: Security was important to the hunter-gatherer, and it is no less so to modern man. By contrast, freedom of information and the right to anonymity will not have troubled our earlier ancestors, though they are important values in today's society. Looking at culture as a whole, we find that some memes are older, others younger.

The vertical arrangement of hexagons on the Culture Map basically follows this logic. Broadly speaking, the older values are below, the newer ones above. But that is not to say that the old values were inferior to the newer ones! Both the hammer and the endoscope are useful tools, though the former was invented some 30,000 years earlier. Which of the two instruments is "better" is strictly a matter of context, of the particular situation. Yet it is also hardly a coincidence that the hammer was invented before the endoscope and not the other way around. In a similar manner, the Culture Map arranges its hexagons in an evolutionary pattern, beginning with purple and going via red and blue to orange, before ending up, via green and yellow, at aqua. A color's values provide the preconditions for the emergence of the next color.

As you will see in the chapters on the colors of the Culture Map, each cluster of colors emerges as an answer to the problems of the previous stage: Red values break through the conformity enforced by purple ones, blue values bring order to red chaos, and so forth. What this does not mean is that blue is better than red or red better than purple. The opposite may be equally true. As with the choice between hammer and endoscope, what counts is context.

The Culture Map

The development of cultural patterns in organizations

Organizations are living organisms in a dynamic
and complex world.

Complexity and interconnectedness call for a holistic view.

A business is a knowledge organization.
Solving problems requires information.

Knowledge is key.

People are a business's most important resource—
and above all, people are people.

A company is only as good as its staff.

Entrepreneurship means recognizing opportunities
and finding practical solutions.

The market is dynamic and customer needs change.

A business organization coordinates tasks and
attains quality by setting standards.

Quality and efficiency are critical for success.

Whoever acts with speed and determination will prevail.

Competition is tough and merciless.

A business is a big family.
Its strength lies in its sense of community.

You're not competitive on your own.

The x-axis: the pendulum

With each step, the hexagons of the Culture Map, and with them, the memes they contain, move to and fro between two poles. These recall the individualist/collectivist dichotomy which Geert Hofstede used to draw intercultural comparisons.[45] On the right side of the Culture Map are the values and attitudes expressing an orientation towards groups or systems. Here, people place common interests in the foreground, their own needs in the background. More self-oriented values and attitudes are found on the left. They foster individual initiative. Unlike the stabilizing right-hand, they ensure dynamics and openness. Community-oriented purple is followed by egocentric red, then come blue, with its obedience to structures, and ambitious orange. Egalitarian green precedes freedom-loving yellow, upon which follows holistic aqua.

As with each individual color, neither axis of the Culture Map is in and of itself good or bad—neither the right-hand side nor the left, neither top nor bottom. The purpose of the two axes is merely to allow for pattern formation, which in turn helps to interpret cultures.

Left-hand side		Right-hand side
Individualism		Collectivism
Self-orientation		Group orientation
Self-confidence		Common identity
Asserting oneself		Humbleness
Will to prevail		Self-sacrifice
Adapting the environment		Adapting to the environment
Opening the group		Strengthening the group
Energizing		Stabilizing
Flexibility		Continuity
Autonomy		Community

Patterns, not categories

The hexagons of the Culture Map should not be mistaken for classes intended to categorize people. Some studies of culture and far more personality tests fall into the trap of putting simple labels on people. Yet what is already evident in describing individuals is all the more clearly so in describing culture: No culture could ever fit a single category.

Many widely used models of culture tend to situate cultural traits along single, one-dimensional scales with contradictory concepts at each end:

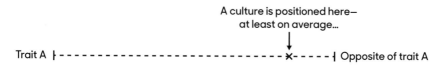

A problem with such models is that two cultures can, by averaging out their scores across variables, end up in the same place along the scale, though one may be homogenous and the other diverse; or two equally large groups may cluster at each extreme.

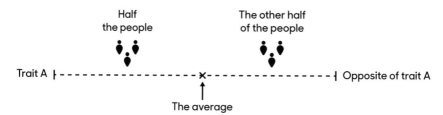

The dichotomies themselves, between which these scales are drawn, are far from being unproblematic. The opposite of "strong" might be "weak," "mild," or "gentle," depending on whether the reference is to a person, a cup of coffee, or a breeze. By the same token, the opposite of a quick decision might be a well-considered, a consensual, or a holistic one, depending on cultural context.

This is not to deny that trying to depict a culture invariably involves a degree of simplification. After all, that is the very reason we use models. Nonetheless, I would like to emphasize that a cultural pattern more closely approximates complex reality than one-dimensional scales or simple labels are able to—and recognizing the pattern is the key.

The Culture Map aims not to reproduce an arithmetical average of a moment's impression, but patterns of a culture's dynamic behaviors. You might compare it with the TV analysis of an important soccer game: Not every yard run is of equal importance in understanding the game. Far more interesting is the pattern that emerges from all these moves taken together. This shows us, which half of the pitch the action was concentrated in, whether play was mostly straight down the middle or along the wings, and if short passes or long kicks predominated.

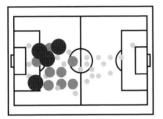 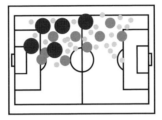 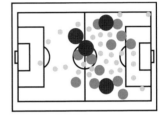

Transferred to corporate culture, this means that reading too much into a detailed snapshot can be deceptive. Even a strongly blue company will surely contain the odd yellow meme. It is only in the pattern that a culture reveals its true character. A little experiment may serve to illustrate this. Take a look at this picture. It's quite possible that you recognize it as a photo of Albert Einstein—as

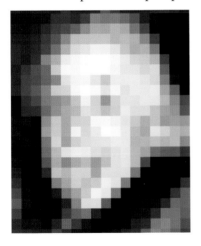

long as you don't let the blurriness distract you. That's the trick. The closer you get to picture, the less you see. Pressing your nose against the screen will leave you seeing nothing but a lot of grey squares. That is the mistake many analytical procedures make: They concentrate on a part of the picture, trying to get ever closer. In this case, however, being able to see just part of the picture would be of little use; in fact, it would be of no help at all in decoding the picture's message. Nor could you reconstruct the picture's essence even if you had all its details at your disposal—all you would see is a collection of squares in shades of grey. Averages, too, will make you none the wiser, for the average is simply grey.

Parts	Details	Average

It is therefore essential to allow for a degree of imprecision in cultural analyses, to take their blurriness into account. Only then do the patterns come into focus. Often, it helps to take a step or two away from the picture in order not to be overwhelmed by details—particularly if what you are facing is not a lot of static grey boxes, but a complex, dynamic system like a business organization.

System in Focus

Naturally, every organization contains not just one culture, but several—subcultures, if you will. As you already know, culture emerges wherever people organize with a purpose in mind. And within the same company, they do so in various settings, for instance in teams or departments.

The existence of subcultures within a culture by no means negates the existence of an overarching culture. Something similar applies to national cultures: It is possible to speak of typically Italian habits and customs, and yet remain aware of cultural differences between northern and southern Italy. Insiders may well be able to discern further subcultures within Lombardy, or point out that the city folk of Milan are in some respects quite unlike their cousins in the surrounding countryside.

Subcultures may also cross other lines. Within Milan, the fashion industry has no doubt developed a set of habits and manners that set it apart from the financial industry, which is quite likely to resemble its London counterpart.

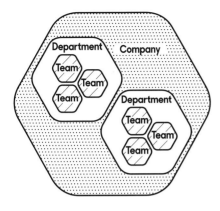

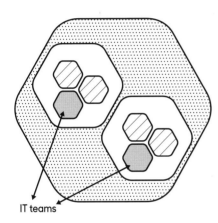

IT teams

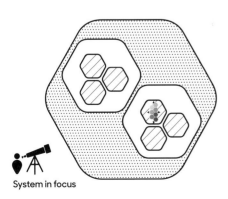

System in focus

By the same token, in a large corporation, the IT team at the head office may well be closer, culturally speaking, to the IT teams at branch offices around the world than to the sales department next door.

The emergence of subcultures under the single roof of an overall corporate culture need not be a problem; to a degree, it is even essential. After all, would you really want accounting to be on exactly the same wavelength as sales? Is it not an advantage that R&D is partly driven by different memes than HR? Within the organism of the company, these departments form sub-organisms, which inevitably develop cultures of their own. Of course, the purpose, structure, and personnel of each sub-organism must be organized in such a way as to contribute to the whole. Subcultures can present a serious problem if they do not develop in harmony with the overall corporate culture. In that case, they are harmful to the organization, because they might seclude themselves in silos or even end up working against the whole.

However, the general rule applies here, too: The extent to which these subcultures are permitted and indeed encouraged to develop independently of the overall corporate culture need not be left to chance, but can be managed: by conscious, purposeful Business Culture Design. In order to do so, it is necessary to decide which "system in focus" to describe when using the Culture Map. After all, you need to know which culture you're talking about.

Healthy or unhealthy?

Humans are creatures of habit. This is evident in the cultural patterns of organizations. Although, theoretically, all colors of the Culture Map could be equally represented, I have yet to witness a corporate culture that did not display a marked preference for "its" colors.

Think back to the comparison with a toolbox in Chapter 1: Every culture has a box with seven drawers for tools, one in each color. Theoretically, it would be entirely possible to use them all. Yet as a rule, we tend to prefer reaching for the same drawers and their familiar tools, especially if they have proved their worth in the past. It must be a part of human nature to try the same thing repeatedly rather than taking a chance on something new.

Whether or not using a particular drawer is good or bad is not something that can be decided in isolation from other factors. No color is inherently better or worse than any other. Yet at the same time, every color can be healthy or unhealthy in its effects. Two aspects in particular are decisive in coming to an assessment: context and extent.

Context

As you will remember from Chapter 2: An organism's success depends on its ability to function in a specific environment. Certain cultural characteristics may be helpful in a particular context, but turn out to be harmful in another. As an airline passenger, you should hope that a resolutely blue culture prevails in the cockpit—one that sets store by check lists, doing things by the book, conscientiousness, and so forth. Solid blue, in this situation, counts for more than yellow creativity or red daring. As an old aviators' proverb has it, "there are old pilots and there are daring pilots. But there are no pilots who are both." Safely landed and in the cab into town, a similar measure of blue on the taxi driver's part would likely drive you to despair. Imagine him running through an exhaustive checklist before going anywhere!

Understanding context is thus indispensable to evaluating cultural traits. Only then is it possible to tell whether the expression of certain colors is healthy or not. The concept of the organization-organism can provide orientation. For besides what a culture can or needs to achieve, people and structures also form part of the context in which a culture develops.

Extent

Looking at the kind of things published on management and leadership, taught in seminars, or proclaimed by opinion-leaders, one thing continues to surprise me. The advice they give is often one-dimensional, always calling for *more* of something or other: *more* teamwork, *more* focus on results, *more* trust, and so on. But what if *more* doesn't equal *better* in every case? Many studies have tried to understand what makes a successful leader. A particularly voluminous one revealed two traits supposedly held in common by leading entrepreneurs: persistence, often despite initial failures, and persuasiveness. No doubt these can be important factors indeed. Yet these very traits are often connected with dramatic failures.[46] Wherever people ignore warning signals and persuade others to do likewise, enormous damage can be done.

There is a turning point, beyond which something otherwise helpful turns into something harmful. Everyone knows that body temperature is an important criterion for the health of our own organism. But nobody would pretend that *more* is necessarily *better*. 98.6°F is a good temperature. Much more or less is a problem. Something similar applies to blood pressure, weight, or height—the optimum is to be found somewhere between the extremes.

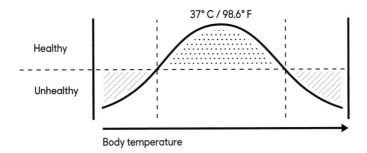

Or, as my grandmother used to say: "It's the dose that makes the poison." Something similar is true of cultural traits. Transparency and teamwork are deservedly valued in organizations. But taken to extremes, transparency can lapse into bureaucracy, and too much teamwork can endanger efficiency.

Applied to the Culture Map: A color owes its dominance to that culture's strengths. But each color has a turning point, past which the hexagon's assets, the more pronounced they become, turn into liabilities. Too much of a good thing turns bad eventually. A little-pronounced hexagon need not be harmful to a culture, for this supposed deficit may, circumstances permitting, be compensated for by other colors. For instance, a low degree of blue formalized organizational structure can, to a degree, be made up for by a purple sense of community.

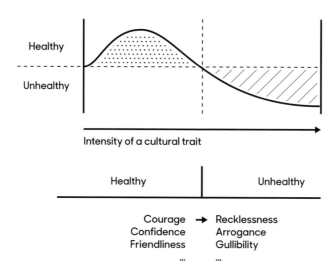

The seven colors of the Culture Map

In this chapter, you will successively immerse yourself in each of the seven colors of the Culture Map. You will find out how the colors of the Culture Map have evolved and how their effects unfold in the business world of today. In reading the following, always bear in mind that the world is a colorful place, and that no culture displays one color exclusively. The complexity of the Culture Map lies in the combination of colors. Nevertheless, it makes sense to begin by considering each color individually, in order better to understand their typology. Treat each color chapter as an ingredient; mixed together, they produce a cultural pattern. The examples given and anecdotes told in the following chapters are intended to illustrate certain aspects of the appropriate color. Yet no organization displays a single, unmixed coloring, and a given example should be understood not as typical or representative of a particular company, but of a color and the memes associated with it.

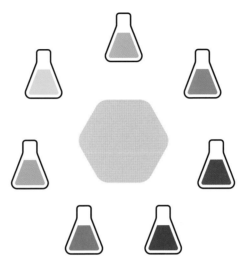

Purple

From Christopher's diary

December 15th

Friday is our traditional Christmas party! For weeks now, decorations have been put up, our products put on display, the company logo everywhere, and even tablecloths in the corporate colors have been ordered! Families are invited, too—like every year.

What we're all anticipating is the chairman's speech. Word is that he'll address the fact that his son and his nephew have both taken on leading positions in the firm over the past year. I wonder how long he will personally remain in charge? For some time yet, we all hope, because he has always maintained continuity. Even in tough times, he never laid off staff. And my father says that old Mr. Cooper used to be just as loyal towards his workforce.

I doubt much will change next year, for me or the company. My own position is unlikely to change—my boss is seven years short of retirement, and I only rose to my position three years ago. Of course I sometimes wonder if I shouldn't have accepted that lucrative offer from a competing firm last year ... but here is where I fit in, where people care about me. And I'm sure my daughter will find a job here too, one day.

So what's to worry about? Our products sell well, we keep growing. Our principle of not going along with every fad, but staying true to our principles, has served us well. Only last week, talk in the cafeteria was about how exaggerated media reports about technological change were. Mark from R&D backed me up on that. The fact that two of his colleagues took a different view and joined the competition clearly shows that they were just after money and never really understood what we're about. After all, they were only with us for two years and never seemed to fit in...

Common strength, strong community

Security is a fundamental human need. People can fulfill this need for each other in communities. Infants know that they are safer in their parents' arms than they would be alone. Even the toughest fans of Liverpool Football Club join in the stirring anthem giving voice to the importance of community: "You'll Never Walk Alone."

The purple memes typical of strong communities recall the tribes formed by our early ancestors to give each other security. To a degree, these memes persist in modern companies: In the community formed by an organization, people can find a sense of belonging, stability, and identity.

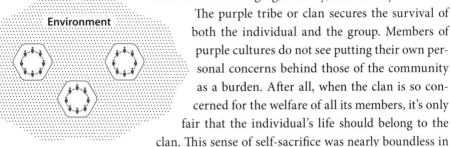

The purple tribe or clan secures the survival of both the individual and the group. Members of purple cultures do not see putting their own personal concerns behind those of the community as a burden. After all, when the clan is so concerned for the welfare of all its members, it's only fair that the individual's life should belong to the clan. This sense of self-sacrifice was nearly boundless in the deeply purple communities of old: The expectations of Aztec kings or pharaohs were particularly high in that regard. Even today, purple cultures consider it highly honorable to make sacrifices for the sake of the community.

In a purple culture, the expectation is that people will behave appropriately. There is the premium on conformity, whereas individual opinions are less welcome. An individual who steps out of line is seen not just as damaging the group's reputation, but also as an instance of collective failure. The group wins and loses together. In sport, players in a purple team compete for the team's victory, not individual glory. What counts is that the team wins! Anyone turning his back on the mutual loyalty of the purple group is considered a traitor. That anybody should renounce the collective and the values it embodies is the cause of severe disappointment. The supporters of FC Barcelona, for instance, were deeply disappointed and extremely angry that their hero, Luis Figo, not only left the club, but then had the temerity to walk onto the pitch in the strip of the arch-rivals, Real Madrid. Amid the deafening whistles, shouted insults, and thrown objects, all the victories he had won with Barcelona were suddenly as nothing. No less deep, if more restrained in its expression, is the sense of grievance felt by purple business leaders when their "star players" sign with the competition. A transfer from McKinsey to Boston Consulting, from Mercedes to BMW, or from Apple to Google can deeply wound a community's pride and sense of honor.

A clear outward boundary

To outsiders, purple companies often seem nearly impenetrable, almost like a secret society or an exclusive club, and reluctant to grant so much as a peek behind their doors. This separation is additionally empha-sized by underscoring the group's homogeneity and difference from others. "We are who we are," as they say in Bavaria, signaling not hostility to others, but identification with that state's traditions and what outsiders may consider to be its peculiarities.

Outsiders are often perceived stereotypically, for there is little interest in a diversified understanding of "the Other," direct contact with whom tends to be avoided. A purple team will always put its members first—and second, third, and fourth … Non-members are outsiders, and that is what they will remain.

In the sign of the cross or the crescent moon, flying the red flag or the Stars & Stripes, under the colors of the rainbow or of a sports team—purple groups proudly present their symbols and thus underscore the presence of a community inwardly and outwardly united by a set of values. In business organizations, this often expresses itself in a strong corporate identity: Everything, from pencils to delivery trucks, is kept in corporate colors. Some companies even have oaths or anthems intended to forge closer links between team members. Songs, too, from military marches via folk tunes to rap tracks, transmit purple memes, as do cer-tain salutations or handshakes. Many rituals that mark life's stages, from baptism to burial, follow traditional and thus purple social patterns. In businesses, such patterns can be discerned in occasions such as anniversaries or award celebra-tions.

Purple memes put a premium on uniformity and homogeneity. In practice, this is often accomplished through dress codes. Uniforms are a particularly striking way of signally group membership to insiders and outsiders. Whether in fast food outlets, schools, or the military—visibly forsaking individuality emphasizes the community's importance.

Even a less rigorously set dress code does not mean that there are no informal guidelines for what to wear in strongly purple workplaces. In this sense, cufflinks in a London law office have the same purpose as hoodies at a Berlin startup: They signal that the wearer is "in." Too individual a sense of style, at variance with the company's norm, would seem willfully confusing.

Outsiders often have a hard time recognizing what certain symbols mean to members of a purple group. To be in possession of a genuine ticket stub to the 1966 World Cup final at Wembley may be of inestimable importance to an English soccer fan, whereas the average American would see little more than a scrap of old paper, the emotional significance of which is completely lost on him. By the same token, an outsider may find a company's symbols and rituals to be faintly ridiculous and sneer at its flags and anthems. Yet being part of a purple culture means not just understanding their significance, but perceiving the derision of others as a threat to one's own identity.

New arrivals to purple firms are usually familiarized early on with the organization's values and customs, in order to avoid any misunderstanding. They pass through a training program or are mentored by "old hands." Initiation rituals can demonstrate arrival in and assimilation to a community. Nonetheless, key positions in purple businesses seldom go to outsiders. Their success elsewhere counts for little against their lack of internal standing and the alliances that come with it. Trusted employees with a track record of loyalty are preferred, for they possess the required internal standing and know the ropes.

Identity connects

Small businesses or startups are naturally endowed with a strong dose of purple: People know each other and thus need no explicitly formulated rules or structures, since all members are aware of the values underlying the operation. Individual roles and positions within the company are far less important than its functioning as a group. Common bonds are enacted on a daily basis, and the boss, exercising authority and solicitude, is a familiar presence. The founder of Airbnb, Brian Chesky, wrote a memo to his staff under the stern heading "Don't Fuck Up the Culture." In it, he emphasizes the purple traits of the corporate culture: "The stronger the culture, the less corporate process a company needs. When the culture is strong, you can trust everyone to do the right thing. [...] Ever notice how families or tribes don't require much process? That is because there is such a strong trust and culture that it supersedes any process."[47]

As a business continues to grow, however, it is not always easy to maintain the positive aspects of a purple culture. Zappos CEO Tony Hsieh recalls the culture of his first company, Link Exchange, which began as a homogeneous group of like-minded friends with no need for formal structures. But the more the business grew, the more it lost of the original spirit: "We had a lot of fun, but then we ran into a really big problem when we got to about 20 people. And the problem was basically that we ran out of friends. [...] And we ended up hiring other people with the right experience and skill sets, but they weren't all necessarily great for the company culture. By the time we got to a hundred people, I myself dreaded getting out of bed in the morning to go to the office."[48]

In his next business, Zappos, Hsieh wanted to avoid this pitfall and devised Zappos as a world unto itself. Its unofficial—but no less strict—dress code consists mostly of t-shirts and sneakers. High-fives and hugs are ubiquitous, as are murals conveying symbolic messages and the tattoos freely displayed by staff. Eyebrows were also raised by Zappos' treatment of new hires: After basic training and a few weeks on the job, new arrivals were offered a bonus of $2,000—if they quit. Hsieh explained the rationale for this move: "We want to make sure that employees are here for more than just a paycheck. We want employees that believe in our long-term vision and want to be a part of our culture."[49]

The company's experience reveals that very few trainees take up this offer. Most of them choose to commit to Zappos and thus to become part of the Zappos culture. Accordingly, the phrase at Zappos is not Work-life-balance, but work-life-*integration*, since living and working are understood as one and the same thing, indissolubly connected. The job becomes part of one's identity, and colleagues form an extended family.

Chieftains with privileges

To people in early tribal communities, a great deal of what happened around them was inexplicable and threatening. The most obvious explanation was that such things must be the work of a higher power. That believing in such a power entails a degree of submission on the individual's part has never been an issue in purple cultures. Especially in times of crisis, faith offers help and direction. It need not even be altogether reasonable. On the contrary, there is a distinct appeal to what eludes our capacity for reason. Experience, one's own as well as that embodied in traditional teachings, counts for a great deal in purple cultures. Yet purple memes by no means restrict belief in a higher power to God or supernatural forces; it can also extend to other people, like an individual able to lead the community—the chieftain.

In a purple group, the chieftain is endowed with a natural authority setting him above the others. To him are ascribed abilities, knowledge, and wisdom not given to the common people. Within the tribe, he thus enjoys an exalted position. "Quod licet Jovi, non licet bovi," as the Romans used to say—to paraphrase: There's one law for the gods, another for the herd. Many in a purple group may consider themselves equals, but not all. Ordinary folk accept this distribution of roles as well as their individual rank in the hierarchy, their function, and their own place in the community. However modest that may be, it is considered infinitely preferable to any position outside the community.

Norms inculcated from childhood may guide the community's behavior, and society as a whole polices adherence, but the leader always is and remains the ultimate source of authority and jurisdiction. He is not expected to justify his decisions, and nobody would dream of objecting—at least not his followers. He is considered to be infallible, and is sure of it himself. To admit to errors is thus difficult and takes time, sometimes centuries. Only in 1992 did Pope John Paul II apologize for his distant predecessor having punished Galileo for claiming that the earth orbited the sun—359 years after Galileo was placed under house arrest on pain of death.

A craving for stability is more pronounced in purple cultures than the desire for change. Leaders frequently owe their elevated position to their exemplary service to the clan, together with a degree of seniority. Belonging to the right family can help, and children can inherit their parents' reputation. Lee Kun-hee, for instance, the son of Samsung's founder, headed the Samsung Group for decades. Inevitably, everyone assumed that he would be succeeded by his children, who had already been groomed in the business. But even after a heart attack, the old chieftain—70 at the time—was loath to surrender his crown and continued to run Samsung from his hospital bed.

Traditional recipes for success

A purple community may have accrued its store of experience over generations, yet the limits of the group also mark the limits of that knowledge. Foreign ideas threaten the security that the purple trove of experience imparts. Such communities have little use for curiosity, scientific interest, or pragmatic experimentation. They prefer to stick to what they know; all the more so if it overlaps with personal experience. A kind of collective memory records experiences and the lessons learned from them. What members of the group lived through generations ago is still present in later minds.

But how, then, does a purple organization learn? At heart, the learning process resembles the classic model of conditioning: A particular stimulus triggers a particular behavior—based on earlier experience. The hows and whys of the matter—causality—barely get a look in. This is equally true of decision-making, in which, alongside experience, the leader's word carries the day: What was right in the past will be no less so in the future. And anyhow, the chieftain is always right.

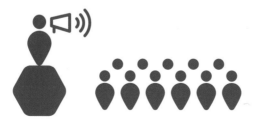

In strongly purple companies, tasks are distributed according to the same principles as resources or profits: in a top-down, patriarchal manner, by seniority (and thus experience), and with the group's welfare in mind. What counts as solidarity in this culture others often regard as nepotism or even corruption. Yet from a purple perspective, what counts is the collective benefit, not individual rewards. Profits are invested in such a manner as to benefit the company. Pay may well be relatively low, but the firm will invest in things that help employees do good work in the long run, like ergonomic chairs and desks, childcare facilities, or bike and car-sharing facilities. Such amenities help make life and work more agreeable for employees.

Decisions are guided by securing the company's long-term existence, not by quick profits or individual advancement. Consider the famous German maker of gummy bears: "Kids and grown-ups love it so, the happy world of Haribo." And they have done so since 1921. The founder's son, Hans Riegel, Jr.—named, of course, after his father, Hans Riegel—was at the helm of the company from 1946 to his death in 2013. Observers agreed that the business and Riegel formed a unit.[50] When rumors began to circulate that Warren Buffett was interested in buying shares in Haribo, Hans Riegel, Jr.—85 at the time—made it perfectly clear that "money was never what drove me. I don't even know by when I made my first million."[51] Of course the patriarch would never have sold his family! The world leader in hinges, Julius Blum, also makes it its paramount principle "to safeguard the company in the long term for its employees"[52]—and it has done so for generations. The principle goes back to the founder, and it continues to guide leaders in their decisions.

A good helping of purple memes can often be found at work in the so-called "hidden champions," the sometimes unsung medium-sized businesses that play so important a part in the German economy. The idea is to keep doing well what one has done well in the past. Instead of bringing revolutionary improvements to their goods and services, purple businesses concentrate on the incremental improvement of their product, one that has existed for years and often decades. This takes continuity and staying power; risk is preferably avoided. For a BBC documentary, the journalist Justin Rowlatt visited an exemplar of such a firm: Faber-Castell, the world leader in pencils and crayons.[53] The company, which employs 7,000 people, goes back centuries, and is led by Anton Wolfgang Graf von Faber-Castell, a descendent of its founder. He underscores its purple traits: "We focus on traditional products, the things we do really well." Rather than losing itself in the complexity of all the things one might do in addition, the company concentrates on perfecting its existing product. Loyalty, identification with the firm, and a long association with it, sometimes beginning with apprenticeship, are due not just to the benefits offered, like subsidized cafeterias or healthcare provided by resident physicians. Their causes run deeper. As Rowlatt found to his surprise, Faber-Castell really does care about "us" first and foremost, which is why the company looks after its employees' wellbeing even after hours. "Family-mindedness" of this kind can pay. Studies have shown that such "hidden champions" are not only good at holding on to employees, their sick rolls are also much smaller.[54]

Unhealthy purple

Stable though a purple organization may seem, dangers lurk beneath the surface. The construct is founded not on objective rule and laws, but on evolved norms and personal sensibilities. Nepotism is far from unusual; knowing the chieftain or even being related to him helps. Cultivating relationships is thus important to advancement. The leader's supposed infallibility can also endanger the community's development. Since criticism, let alone objections, is forbidden in the decision-making process, bad decisions become apparent only when they are virtually irreversible. To the bitter end, the purple chieftain's infallibility goes unquestioned.

On the whole, purple cultures don't much care for change. The focus is decidedly inward, with the effect that changes in the environment are barely perceived. And even if they are, reasons are at hand to carry on as before. "Morality binds and blinds," says the social psychologist Jonathan Haidt. He explains that "one of the most important principles of morality is that morality binds and blinds. It binds us into teams that circle around sacred values but thereby makes us go blind to objective reality."[55] To purple communities, things are the way they are—and life is the way it is. Alternative viewpoints are not considered. To revolve around existing values engenders stability.

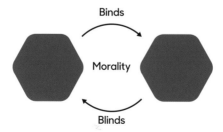

76   Business Culture Design

Nor do purple communities always succeed in an optimum distribution of tasks, responsibilities, and rewards. Purple memes can actually obstruct performance and deter high performers. Good and dedicated employees may leave if they find the company culture constantly standing in the way of their ideas. Few people likely to take an opposite view are attracted to the purple faith, and fewer still are accepted. Young employees in particular have a hard time brining their potential to bear in purple organizations. New ideas are likely to fall on deaf ears, especially if they are introduced by somebody who has not yet gained appropriate standing by having put in many years with the firm.

Additionally, the low level of autonomy enjoyed by individuals not only stifles initiative, but also individual responsibility. Employees in purple cultures learn that responsibility rests with the collective. So instead of taking their fate into their own hands, group members prefer to rely on others—especially the chieftain. The individual feels neither the right nor the obligation to display initiative or suggest changes. Coupled with the risk-averseness typical of purple cultures, this can lead to stagnation and ultimately endanger the organization's future.

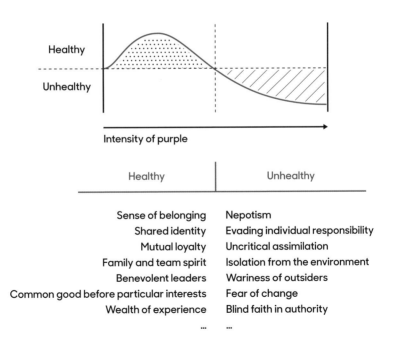

Healthy	Unhealthy
Sense of belonging	Nepotism
Shared identity	Evading individual responsibility
Mutual loyalty	Uncritical assimilation
Family and team spirit	Isolation from the environment
Benevolent leaders	Wariness of outsiders
Common good before particular interests	Fear of change
Wealth of experience	Blind faith in authority
...	...

Red

From Martin's diary

December 15th

Damn, what an amazing day! Tough, but ultimately victorious—again.
The boss called first thing. Gave me hell about China. Told him his strategy was wrong. He didn't like that one bit. Whatever, I'm going through with this. I'm not backing down.

Then, in the team meeting, I set the juniors right. I only slept for four hours, and these kids come up with lame excuses for all the things that supposedly won't work. Peter presented his concept—way too theoretical, too complicated. He won't make it past probation. Now Shirley, on the other hand— there's a tough cookie. She'll go far. Just look at how she faced up to George last Friday—totally fearless. Hats off. (Note to self: Watch out, she's as mean as a snake!)

At midday, a meeting in the war room: Operation "sales plus 30" is totally working out! We pulled it out of nowhere and completely steamrollered the competition. They're still at the drawing board while we're cleaning up the market. Mission accomplished. So they may come up with a better-developed product in six months' time, but that'll be too late for them. The momentum is on our side. By then, we'll have the market standing and the cash just to buy them up!

In the management meeting, Paul got such crap for that business about the warranty lawsuits—from everyone! He won't last long. And when he's finally gone, I'll take over his department. High time somebody mixed things up there. I'm all geared up!

Business Culture Design

Mine, all mine!

The security and stability that purple groups offer their members places severe restrictions on personal freedom. Sooner or later, people will begin to question the secure, but far from self-determined, way of life. The result is a longing for autonomy and individuality. Infected with red memes, people become bolder and brasher—like pubescent teenagers challenging parental authority, which they previously accepted and indeed appreciated. Suddenly, they come to recognize the weaknesses of authorities which turn out not to be so infallible after all, and question their rules as well as those of society at large.

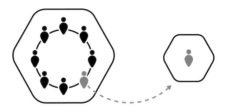

Red memes preserve people from conforming to and accepting the world as it is. Time and again, they seek to break through seemingly fixed boundaries. Decisive historical events display strong evidence of red memes: the French Revolution, the student protests of 1968, and the Arab Spring, no less than Solidarność or WikiLeaks. One of the most famous redheads of children's literature and TV, Pippi Longstocking, was introduced with the lines "Freedom calls and Pippi runs / The girl who never heard she couldn't do something." In the stories by Astrid Lindgren, the buccaneer's daughter successfully defies social norms, the forces of order, and, of course, her teachers.

Often fighting alone, reds break with stale structures and habits, are unafraid of conflict, and display courage and conviction in taking on the establishment. This requires a strong spirit. Their individualism wreaks havoc among familiar group structures. And it soon becomes clear: The world *can* be changed! This realization reinforces their self-confidence and faith in the individual's seemingly infinite potential.

Naturally, the distribution of power, property, and wealth in strongly red cultures is quite uneven. Equality prevails only inasmuch as everybody takes what he can get. This instinct is held in great esteem. Whereas, in purple cultures, power is legitimized by past services or affiliations, red cultures adhere to the principle "might makes right." Anyone successfully enacting power will find right on his side. The only way of avoiding being oppressed is to build and extend one's own power, and not be unduly concerned with collateral damage in the process. Accordingly, growth is the primary aim. Nor does it have to be organic: takeovers, friendly or hostile, form an integral part of red business strategy.

Little wonder that not everybody is comfortable when red memes come to play in an organization. But that's not to say that they are inherent unhealthy for businesses—on the contrary. What the Austrian economist Joseph Schumpeter famously referred to as "creative destruction"[56] cannot occur without a good deal of red, for only breaking through established patterns and structures allows creativity and innovation to unfold.

By hook or by crook

Limits is not a word to be found in a red organization's vocabulary. Doubt or excessive caution? Never heard of them. Emotions are instantly translated into action. Decisions are made by gut feeling and are final. If the result is running into a wall, then the attempt is simply repeated—just more forcefully. The rule is: If force doesn't work, more force just might. In any case, giving up is not an option. Nor is taking a deep breath and pausing to consider the best possible solution the red way. Red energy and resolve can move mountains. As Peter Drucker put it so memorably, "Ideas don't move mountains, bulldozers move mountains."[57] And red imagines itself as such a bulldozer.

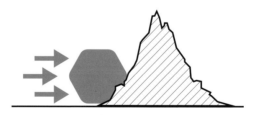

Especially in times of crisis, red traits and values are vital. When Sergio Marchionne took the helm at Fiat, which was struggling at the time, he imposed on that traditional corporation a culture that consistently questioned everything and moved much faster. Marchionne resolutely overturned bureaucratic processes and time-honored habits. With typical red openness, he let his leaders-to-be know what was expected of them: "It's not the Buena Vista Social Club. [...] But if you like being truly engaged; if you like big, bold objectives; if you don't mind taking risks, this is the perfect place to be."[58]

A mellow Cuban atmosphere was as little in evidence at General Electric under Jack Welch. Through a painful process of restructuring, he led the giant corporation to new growth. His foremost principle, for many years, was "intolerance for bureaucracy," and the CEO called on staff to "to 'blow up' bureaucracy and knock down every boundary,"[59] Under Welch's leadership, General Electric abandoned many an old habit and took on a new dynamic. When deciding on acquisitions, he valued gut instinct higher than "some silly calculation."[60] He was pitiless in personnel decisions and soon earned the moniker "Neutron Jack,"[61] after the neutron bomb: designed to leave buildings intact while eliminating their inhabitants. Every year, Welch fired the lowest-performing ten per cent of his managers, regardless of how good a year it had been; the best, meanwhile, were rewarded with bonuses and stock options.

Jack Welch always maintained that "business is simple." Too many rules are seen as restrictive in red organizations. Nor are there detailed job descriptions, handbooks, or codes of conduct. There is little patience for long planning processes, preparatory meetings, and the like. Red organizations are impatient and raring to go. Tasks at hand are outlined as briefly as possible, because it is quite clear how the job is to be done: quickly, with full commitment, and let the chips fall as they may. While other businesses may still be bent over strategic plans or product specifications, the red company has already leapt into action. At such a speed, there is little time for putting up safety nets or having second thoughts. Testing and trials are kept to a minimum; the premium is on speed. "Done is better than perfect,"[62] reads a banner at Facebook's HQ—a clear message from the red meme brigade. The idea is to learn on the job, live and in real time. While the established TV networks were still fine-tuning their online strategies, Netflix built up a globally operating streaming service. Its CEO, Reed Hastings, proudly summarized the values driving him and his staff. "Courage" is one of them—Netflix explicitly demands its employees make "tough decisions," "take smart risks," and "say what [they] think even if its is controversial."[63] Emboldened by its red memes, Netflix took on not just the video rental trade, but the entire film and TV industry—remaking it in the process.

Nothing's impossible

If you enter www.relentless.com into your web browser, you will be redirected to amazon.com. "Relentless" is what Jeff Bezos wanted to call his company before going for the world's largest and longest river instead. Even in the mid-1990's, hardly anyone could imagine buying things on the internet. No properly worked-out business case would have justified betting everything on online retail. Established retailers thus were in no hurry to act. Bezos, on the other hand, acting with daring and tenacity, conquered a world into which others dared not venture. He fought relentlessly indeed.

People who used to work with Steve Jobs recount how they nearly despaired of his "Reality Distortion Field," his incredible willpower that many found to be divorced from reality.[64] Jobs lived in a world of his own. He wasn't too bothered about sticking to the facts, regardless whether the issue was historical dates, paternity tests, or whether an idea really was his own or had been introduced to him by someone else. Whenever reality collided with his own truth, he relied on his version of things—in which there were no limits. This allowed him to change the world of computing forever, though others, like IBM or Xerox, had more resources at their disposal. Jobs's confidant Bud Tribble remembers: "It was dangerous to get caught in Steve's distortion field, but it was what led him to actually be able to change reality."[65]

It was thus that a culture emerged in which people could make possible the impossible—because "impossible" was not a concept their CEO had any time for. That nothing was above being changed was also the creed of Jordan Belfort, the ace stockbroker who was later portrayed in the movie *The Wolf of Wall Street*. "Successful people are 100% convinced that they are masters of their own destiny, they're not creatures of circumstance, they create circumstance, and if the circumstances around them suck, they change them."[66] Even after the law had made him painfully aware of the limits and he spent several years in jail, he made his comeback as a motivational coach, his faith in the power of the individual unbroken: "The only thing standing between you and your goal is the bullshit story you keep telling yourself as to why you can't achieve it."[67] That he nearly drowned because he set sail in his yacht in the midst of a strong gale—against his captain's advice—proves that he takes his own advice seriously. Red to the bone, he won't take no for an answer, not even from an expert.

To red organizations, the marketplace is a battlefield, and competitors are enemy forces. Red leaders like using the imagery of warfare when rallying their troops. If they lose a battle, they react angrily. Steve Jobs left no doubt how Apple intended to react to Google's launch of Android: "I will spend my last dying breath if I need to, and I will spend every penny of Apple's $40 billion in the bank, to right this wrong. I'm going to destroy Android, because it's a stolen product. I'm willing to go to thermonuclear war on this."[68]

The red alarm is always on a hair-trigger—quite literally so, considering that *alarm* derives from the French call to arms: "À l'arme!" Believing that attack is the best defense, preventative strikes are an integral part of the red repertoire. A leaked e-mail reveals Oliver Samwer, co-founder of the incubator Rocket Internet, summoning his staff to a "blitzkrieg": "The only thing is that the time for the blitzkrieg must be chosen wisely, so each country tells me with blood when it is time. I am ready—anytime!"[69] The choice of words ensures that the message is understood, its slightly awkward English notwithstanding. Samwer proudly describes himself as "the most aggressive man on the internet," and few would doubt his pledge: "I would die to win."

Red organizations fear nothing except the humiliation of defeat or of cowardice. Better to go under than to bear that shame! And should defeat ensue in spite of all efforts, red cultures are quick to find scapegoats.

Hell-bent commanders

Alexander the Great, a red hero if ever there was, spent most his rule trying to conquer the world. Full of daring and resolve, he led his troops from Macedonia to India, ready to do battle with anybody who would stop him. He untied the legendary Gordian knot in classic red style: with his sword.

At the head office of Chinese corporation Haier, now the world's largest producer of household appliances, a sledgehammer is prominently exhibited as a memento of a crucial period in the company's history.[70] When Zhang Ruimin took over as CEO in 1984, the company was close to ruin. The new CEO found serious problems with quality. Many refrigerators were broken before they were even delivered. Zhang gathered his workers around a batch of refrigerators awaiting delivery, picked up a sledgehammer, and smashed one of them, then told his workforce to do likewise. There can hardly be a more memorable or aggressive way of making one's point: Poor quality is unacceptable!

Red leaders have no qualms about regularly demonstrating their power. They leave no doubt that they would do anything to hold on to their position. By the same principle, the second tier rules over the third, and so forth. In the early modern age, Machiavelli taught and practiced red values. In the eyes of this Italian philosopher and politician, power was essential, mistrust natural, and violence an appropriate means to an end. In his book, *The Prince*, he taught rulers that, after having weighed all the arguments, "it is far safer to be feared than loved."[71]

Red rulers demonstrate their authority at every level. For they know: Any power vacuum would immediately be filled by someone else. To accept power relations in which other people have more power than oneself is difficult for people in red cultures. Obedience to the current ruler is given reluctantly, and the task is to build up one's own power in order to turn the tables.

The aim of behavior in red cultures is always to avoid being limited, let alone dominated, by others. To that end, do what you must. It's a jungle out there, and surviving means fighting. That's the nature of things. Only the strongest prevail, you win or you are vanquished. What is equally clear is that it is better to be the strong conqueror than to be conquered because of one's own weakness. Consequently, the defeated have no right to complain. Pity the losers? No way! Frank Underwood, the Machiavellian protagonist of the Netflix show *House of Cards*, knows all the red tricks:[72]

Every kitten grows up to be a cat. They seem so harmless at first—small, quiet, lapping up their saucer of milk. But once their claws get long enough, they draw blood, sometimes from the hand that feeds them. For those of us climbing to the top of the food chain, there can be no mercy. There is but one rule: hunt or be hunted.

Underling or potential threat?

For a red commander, there are two types of employee. The first is remarkably similar to himself; both leader and follower play by the same book. As a result, there is much mutual distrust, for such employees are ambitious and thus dangerous. The other kind is obviously not red and thus, in the eyes of his superior, weak, or lazy, or both. The boss must lead such people with a rod of iron if results are to be expected.

Business Culture Design

Hence, the "stick and carrot" approach is a widespread red leadership style. The stick is a handy way of keeping people in line. Rewards to keep employees greedily snapping for new prey are the carrot in this image. Learning is thus triggered by the prospect of immediate rewards. A finger pointed at the territory to be conquered and the prospect of keeping part of the spoils usually constitutes motivation enough. Abstract lessons are perceived as boring; red cultures value book learning and good advice distinctly less than learning by doing.

Red instructions are clear orders. Compromise is unusual, as is bottom-up decision-making. The addressee of a command has recourse neither to excuses nor to objections—his job is to execute the order. In doing so he is, by the same token, free to choose the means required, including making the same demands of his inferiors. If he is successful, he receives a share of the spoils; if not, he is punished. Steering behavior in red cultures is as simple as that. Rewards must be given immediately and in clear connection with specific results. A red salesman expects his bonus right after the massive deal has been signed, not at the end of year.

What counts is instant gratification—not what may or may not happen in the distant future. Wealth is spent impulsively and conspicuously, without planning ahead or putting something aside for leaner days. Life is lived in the present, entirely in the here and now. As the philosopher Schopenhauer said: "The present is all that is real and everything else merely imaginary."[73] It is this present that red memes inhabit.

On the other hand, punishment in red cultures does not necessarily bring about a change in behavior, but as often as not leads to disputes. Even gentle, diplomatic language is counterproductive in such circumstances, and warnings coupled with negative consequences some time in the future are completely meaningless. Only true commanders, whose power rests on solid foundations, can dispense effective punishments: quickly, decisively, and forcefully, Navy Seals-style, as it were, without letting any doubt arise as to the leader's authority. Nonetheless, the culprit may not show remorse, let alone be troubled by his conscience.

In red cultures, employees accept their superior's power of them for better or for worse—as long, that is, as he wields it. Should his attention wander and his authority crumble as a result, revolution is not far off. Kindly and gentle leaders in red organizations have a hard time of it.

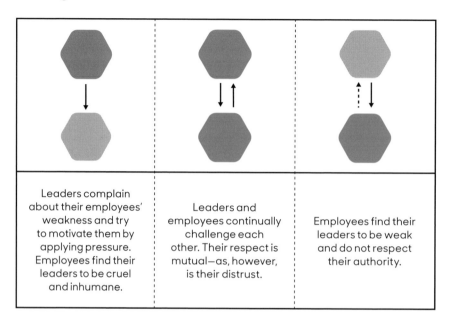

| Leaders complain about their employees' weakness and try to motivate them by applying pressure. Employees find their leaders to be cruel and inhumane. | Leaders and employees continually challenge each other. Their respect is mutual—as, however, is their distrust. | Employees find their leaders to be weak and do not respect their authority. |

The war of all against all

From a red perspective, cooperation only makes sense if there is a short-term payoff for the individual or it helps in fighting a larger common enemy. Reds live by the rule: if you're not for me, you must be against me. Under such circumstances, sober discussions are unlikely. Criticism is likely to meet with impulsive emotional reactions. People don't hide their opinion here. But that also means that anyone wanting to stand up to the boss in a heated debate can do so only in an equally aggressive manner. A polite and softly-spoken expert may have all the facts on his side, but he has no chance of being heard, let alone changing minds.

Life in red organizations, then, is anything but a walk in the park. At the base of the red organization's pyramid are the anonymous foot soldiers. They

Business Culture Design

do the grunt-work. Time was when they shoveled coal on a steamship, now they spend their days and nights coding for an IT company, analyzing data in a consultancy, or building models for an architect. These are tough jobs, and many leave before they have a chance of promotion. Employees are considered as resources in a fairly conventional way. That many are consumed does not figure as a problem; after all, there is no shortage of willing replacements drawn by the allure of rewards and a glittering career. No tears are shed for those who fall by the wayside, since they obviously were too weak to thrive in such a harsh climate.

It is not uncommon for new members to prove their courage, fearlessness, and strength. Such different organizations as a gang in South Central L.A. and a New York investment bank have this in common: Acceptance is won by "showing balls," the value of which is intuitively understood by both.

Employees attracted by red organizations by and large want to make their way by asserting themselves, both inwardly and outwardly. They are resolute and merciless in pursuit of their careers. They know they aren't going to have an easy time of it, nor do they expect it. What they do expect is the opportunity to prove their worth and get ahead. That's what they burn for. The toughest climb the ladder, rung by rung. Though pressure from above may be enormous, they soon learn how to pass it on to their own inferiors—and they show no compunction in doing so.

Unhealthy red

All against all, no time for a breather, no coordination, no rules—this can all too easily end in chaos. The constant struggle in the here and now can obstruct the view of long-term consequences. A victory now may return to haunt reds, especially if the defeated customer, business partner, or colleague decides to leave the red game.

You will search in vain for a choice of courses of action or compromises in red cultures. Nor is there much call for tactics or a "wait-and-see" approach; action is preferably fast and decisive. To hesitate along the path one has taken and to reflect isn't part of the red battle plan either—and plans are generally disdained, as evidenced by the wasteful attitude to resources.

Everybody in the company is bent on consolidating and expanding power. Infighting is far from unusual, and conflicts are fought in the open, even if they do not serve to advance a shared objective. Red organizations lack reliability and trust not just in interpersonal relationships, but also in coordinating processes. Agreements and rules count for little. On the contrary: to push against them counts as a virtue.

A core problem in red organizations is lack of loyalty. In self-centered battles, the welfare of colleagues is of little consequence, as is that of the organization as a whole. But not everybody is willing to fight for survival in red battles. Many talented employees might give strongly red organizations a wide berth—proving, from the red perspective, only to be too feeble for the job.

Finally, the quality of a company's performance is also adversely affected by a lack of foreseeability and order. Coordinated results become impossible amid an impulsive, uncoordinated mess. It really is a chaotic jungle out there, in an unhealthy red organization.

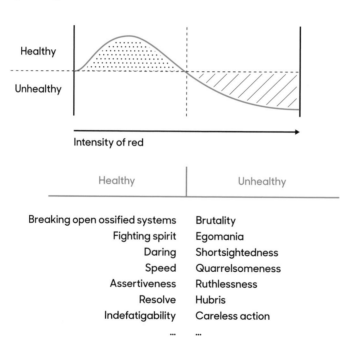

Healthy	Unhealthy
Breaking open ossified systems	Brutality
Fighting spirit	Egomania
Daring	Shortsightedness
Speed	Quarrelsomeness
Assertiveness	Ruthlessness
Resolve	Hubris
Indefatigability	Careless action
...	...

Blue

From Susan's diary

Wednesday, December 15th, 2.35 pm

1. Today, the Coordinating Committee met to discuss phase 2b of the dam project:
   a. I presented the plans for the installation of the turbines. Discussion centered on Milestone 4. To proceed, we need resources from Peter's team, but it is not authorized and has not yet received the go-ahead to support us.
   b. The changes desired by the client, which were raised at the last meeting on November 22nd, are to be evaluated by a working group before being presented for approval to the board next week. This entails a deviation from standard procedure and the associated risk of jeopardizing quality.
2. The new guidelines on composing emails have now been in force throughout the firm for two weeks. Our department has successfully implemented them, but—once again—sales is making trouble by repeatedly ignoring the memos circulated on the subject. The usual suspects are at fault—the same ones who implemented the new meeting protocol incompletely just a few months ago. They have already been reprimanded for that.
3. My annual performance assessment interview takes place tomorrow. I think I have fulfilled my tasks well, and this is confirmed by the "Work Review and Evaluation System" introduced by HR. Last year, I had a fulfillment rate of 95% in six out of seven assessment areas. Since my job description has not changed since, I expect even better results this year.
4. The office of employee deployment planning, attached to HR, has offered me an extra day's vacation next week, since my work time account is showing a surplus that must be removed within two months. These 12.5 hours of overtime accrued in phase 2a of the project.

Law and order

The red jungle leads to anarchy and chaos. Sooner or later, even the victors tire of the constant red battles. Studies reveal that, particularly in troubled times, people yearn for hierarchical structures.[74] When they feel a lack of personal control, they look for order and reliability in their environment. Blue memes are the forces that introduce structure to chaos, tidy up and organize.

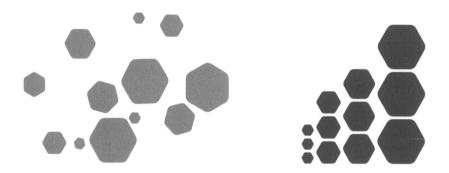

In *Leviathan*, one of the most celebrated works of political philosophy, Thomas Hobbes (1588–1679) proposed a model of society in which blue memes can clearly be discerned. Writing at a time of civil war in his native England, Hobbes found human beings to be engaged in a state of permanent war of "all against all," to which only a strong sovereign and a well-ordered government could put a stop. Each individual was to surrender power and freedom, in return for which the system would guarantee protection and the rule of law.

Blue memes ensure that human behavior is guided not by spontaneous impulses in the here and now, but by long-term, future-oriented planning. Individuals prefer to keep in the background and subordinate themselves to the institution, setting diligence and obedience above their personal desires. At first sight, this may seem reminiscent of purple cultures, but unlike the purple clan, blue groups are held together not by family ties, but by the structure of their formal organization. People feel loyalty to an impersonal institution which, in return, offers them stability and predictability. Its generally accepted and valid rules promise reliability. Subordination is thus understood not as an act of renunciation, but as an achievement on the part of the system.

Business Culture Design

Organizing Organizations

With the advent of mass production in the early 19th century, industrial giants emerged of a kind the world had not yet encountered. Blue memes spread throughout factories and head offices. Single-product firms managed by their owners gave way to major industrial organizations, whose coordination by a central steering instance increasingly came up against its limits.

This industrial system had fully developed by the turn of the 20th century, when the sociologist Max Weber (1854–1920) described bureaucracy as the most efficient and rational form of organization.[75] Though the term "bureaucracy" is unlikely to arouse much excitement anymore—least of all in businesses—Weber's thoughts represented an advance in economic thinking at the time. Among Weber's arguments was that the systematic allocation of resources by an institutionalized, impersonal bureaucracy produced better results than charismatic leadership by individuals, especially where questions of accuracy, stability, reliability, and discipline were at stake. An organization ought thus to be grouped around official functions tied to rules and clearly defined competencies, and themselves be hierarchically structured.

In the 1920s, blue memes influenced up-and-coming corporations like DuPont, General Motors, General Electric, or Standard Oil in their transitions from centralized innovators to companies with multi-divisional structures, organized by product and region.[76] Whereas Ford still traded as a single-product company, Alfred Sloan Jr. introduced a new organizational structure at General Motors, creating "divisions"[77] within the company. With divisions such as Buick, Cadillac, and Pontiac, GM set out the path that would lead it to be the world's largest car manufacturer. The operative units had clearly defined rights. Top management coordinated divisions, allocated budgets and resources, and controlled the corporation as a whole.

Not just at General Motors did a reliable order lay the foundations for efficiency and scalability. Komosuke Matsushita, founder of the eponymous electronics giant better known by its Panasonic brand, also recognized the usefulness of blue memes in management early on. His goal was to turn his innovative inventions into mass-market products. They were to be produced in large quantities, in high quality, and at low prices. In the 1930s, when it became clear that well-coordinated mass production was the key to success, he declared: "the goal of corporations should be to produce all products as plentifully and as cheaply as tap water."[78]

A place for everything, everything in its place

Organizing organizations is what blue memes want. The way a business functions takes priory, rather than individuals with their personal feelings, goals, or preferences. At the heart of blue-dominated organizations is a set of parameters coordinating people and activities. Unsurprisingly, organization charts are particularly popular in blue cultures. They order and classify individuals and departments. They represent hierarchies and relationships as they are supposed to be within the company. And of course blue cultures adhere to these rules. Somebody needing something from another department will follow the official path rather than simply making a connection diagonally through the organization. To leave the designated path or to take short cuts would mean to infringe upon the rules.

Category by category, the blue order is transparent and comprehensible. As a rule, positions within the company are clearly distinguished, for instance by title or job description. What is more, every job, every position comes with a detailed set of instructions. They are taken very seriously in blue organizations because they leave no doubt as to what needs to be done. What is not part of the job description must be somebody else's responsibility. To involve oneself in areas beyond that which has been specifically defined as one's own is neither desired nor permitted in blue organizations.

Positions with a sense of duty

Unlike in purple and red cultures, blue power resides not in a *person*, but in a *position*. A blue leader has no need for charisma, his position automatically confers authority on him. The leader leads *ex officio*, as it were, and the blue system endows the office with authority, rights, but also duties.

Both horizontally and vertically, the patterns of order are unambiguous. In a blue company, nobody takes surreptitious upward or sideways glances, but

Business Culture Design

finds fulfillment in his or her position. Each rank is assigned different tasks and responsibilities; power relations and the chain of command are likewise transparent and universally accepted. It will come as no surprise that many blue memes are to be found in the military, often in combination with red ones: New recruits swear allegiance to a code of conduct. Besides clear hierarchical structures, standards of dress, uniform, and haircut all display a blue imprint. Here, too, the chain of command is accepted as unquestioningly as the rights and duties of each position.

Well-oiled cogs in a machine

With his doctrine of scientific management, Frederick Taylor introduced many blue memes into the workplace. He thought little of uncoordinated experimentation or rules of thumb—he went in search of the *one* right way to organize work. Taylor's approach is built around high levels of standardization and the splitting of large undertakings into small, simple tasks that are easily described and controlled. There was no room in Taylor's production process for critical thinking on the workers' part, let alone independent initiative. On the contrary: Workers were to follow their instructions to the letter and reliably perform the defined tasks they had been allocated.

Companies with a strongly blue culture resemble technical constructions. In the best case, they work like well-oiled machines: Ever cog is reliable, and runs smoothly and tirelessly. Everybody knows what is to be done, and all, managers and staff alike, do their clearly delineated jobs according to plan. Interaction in blue companies is not left to chance, but occurs at designated nodes. This requires considerable discipline on the individual's part. At the end of this process, the overall result holds few surprises.

Individual departure from set tasks, as Charlie Chaplin's assembly line worker in the movie *Modern Times*,[79] causes them, can lead to far-reaching complications in tightly structured blue processes: Chaplin's character works under high pressure and constant surveillance. He has only a few monotonous motions to make, but the speed of the assembly line and the rigorous timing of the production process do not admit the slightest deviation. Just quickly scratching himself causes him to drop the beat and throw the entire machinery off kilter. Spontaneous discussions with his foreman and an insect buzzing around his face provide further distractions, each one felt further down the line.

Sober and dutiful

Blue memes order life and work by rules and regulations. To this end, they define "the one right way," that is to say the modes of conduct designed to keep events under control. Shades of grey or room for interpretation are not part of this plan. The set rules are precisely formulated and, above all, permanent—they do not change according to the whims of the powerful, as purple norms or red commands may do. Blue rules are set in stone, and everybody is obliged to respect them. If a cellphone rings during a meeting, although rules are in place that stipulate that phones must be turned off before the meeting begins, there is little chance of this event passing unremarked in a meeting room full of blue memes. Penalties are set for breaking rules, which may range from an extra contribution to the holiday party fund to being excluded from the meeting.

Blue faith in hierarchies is also evident in learning patterns: Higher positions are obeyed. Knowledge coming from above is possessed of authority, is respected and accepted. Learning long texts by heart and reciting them accurately? No big deal in a blue culture.

Endurance and a sense of duty are blue virtues. Such conscientiousness makes people tenacious in pursuit of their goals: Once begun, they will see a project through. But make no mistake: Such tenacity is quite unlike red stubbornness. Red life resembles a boxing match whereas the blue is more like a marathon. Blue cultures do not try to reach their goals by surprise attacks and brute force, but by persistency, however time-consuming and onerous the task may be. There is a huge potential for quality in this blue trait, for persistency is coupled with consistency, meaning that nobody will settle for less than the prescribed standard. Each step is carried out to the millimeter. Volker Schiek, managing director of a mechatronics industry body in south-western Germany, knows the blue patterns ingrained in the culture of German mechanical engineers with all their strengths and weaknesses: "We often take longer than others to recognize fundamental shifts in markets or technology. But once we've got the message, all wheels are set in motion. With our skills, from the apprentice to

Business Culture Design

the engineer, we are often able to deliver innovative and reliable products ahead of the competition."[80]

Not just employees, but leaders and indeed senior management strive for stability in a blue culture. The interplay of positions and processes is well balanced, and nobody wants to risk disturbing this harmonious, almost mechanical functioning. If adjustments should prove necessary, formal positions are accorded higher importance than the people occupying them. Blue reorganizations thus take little account of personal sensitivities, but rather of organizational schemes. It is only the blue desire for stability that stands in the way of people being readily substituted—after all, that too might be a source of disorder.

Emotions do not generally have much of a role to play in blue cultures—professionalism counts for far more. People do not chase after immediate satisfaction, but trust that it will come in due course. Where red is profligate, blue is thrifty. Red urges are contained by a strict code of conduct and ingrained feelings of guilt. "Better safe than sorry" is one rule by which blue cultures live; another is that no vice goes unpunished. Modesty, hard work, and self-discipline thus become cardinal virtues. Leaders, in particular, ought to face the responsibilities bestowed on them with humility, and conduct themselves in a manner befitting their position. Germany's former chancellor (1974–1982), the late Helmut Schmidt, revealed a thoroughly blue understanding of his office in one of his last TV interviews. Eschewing political romanticism or grand visions, he let objectivity, sobriety, a sense of duty, and clear thinking be his guides.[81] Not by chance was one of the first triumphs of his political career bringing order to chaos after the North Sea flooded his native Hamburg in 1962. Looking back at his life in public office, he concluded: "I would like to be remembered as somebody who accepted his tasks and fulfilled his duties."

Predictable steps and no mistakes

By and large, blue memes are much appreciated in organizations with a low tolerance for mistakes. In aviation, for instance, language is strongly standardized to avoid misunderstanding. Not only is the phonetic alphabet used for spelling, but three is pronounced *tree* and nine *niner* in order to reduce potential confusion. Entire phrases are standardized as "voice procedure" to this end, maximizing clarity and removing ambiguity, no matter who is speaking. And no matter how often a pilot may have flown a particular route: He will always stick to his checklists and standard procedures. Passengers will appreciate the high proportion of blue memes on the flight deck. It may seem monotonous, but a pilot who conscientiously cleaves to protocol is surely preferable to one who regards a scheduled flight as a place to exercise his creativity.

There should be as little room for surprises in aviation as in building bridges or supervising a nuclear power plant. Wherever risk avoidance has top priority, the blue urge towards maximum security comes into its own. The vagaries of the future are prepared for by minute planning—step by step, from one milestone to the next, sequential and linear. In the blue project plan, tasks, responsibilities, and powers are clearly allocated.

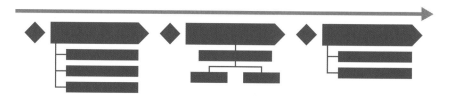

Many of the working techniques that have found their way onto factory floors across the world as the Toyota Production System are decidedly blue in character.[82] Avoiding waste is the goal of the Muda principle, while Poka-Yoke provides technical means for avoiding human error. The 5S method provides a structured working environment by tidying up factories as well as offices. In a workplace organized according to 5S, each tool has its clearly defined and visually indicated place. The Toyota System underlies the Japanese corporation's reputation for quality and its rise to becoming the world's largest manufacturer of motor vehicles. Meanwhile, these blue memes have been adopted not only by other car makers, but also in many other manufacturing industries—and even in offices, where 5S assigns every mouse and every pencil a place on the desk.

Some blue elements find their way not just into the automobile industry or established engineering firms. Even many a creative hothouse keen on giving an outward appearance of informality is not above deploying well-placed blue practices. Quite a few successful artists and other creative minds run their studios by highly professional standards, on tight schedules, strict budgets, and a clear distribution of tasks. And even seemingly spontaneous "reality" TV shows are more often than not scripted.

Reliable Control

Naturally, the individual cogs in the great machinery of the organization cannot be expected to keep in sight the big picture. Blue business cultures thus rely on strong coordination and control from above. Instructions are given top-down, and are followed as long as they are transparent and in accordance with the established rules. Gut decisions or instructions seemingly given on a whim are far less likely to be accepted.

Personal initiative is generally unwelcome in markedly blue cultures, and the scope for individual action is small. Employees and their leaders expect continuity and consistency from each other. If doubts arise as to the interpretation of the rules, appeal is made to above for clarification. Staff expect clear instructions congruent with existing rules. Empty talk on the leader's part is seen as an irritant, and to change existing rules for no good reason is unlikely to find favor in blue cultures. Agreements are treated as having the force of law. And although a man is expected to be as good as his word, the written word is strongly preferred—clearly structured of course, with numbers and bullet points. Blue cultures like to make things explicit and official.

In strongly blue organizations, working time is logged to the minute by electronic systems. Performance reviews make use not just of a set of official guidelines, but also a standardized matrix for evaluating performance transparently, according to fixed criteria—everything done by the book and thoroughly documented. Career paths are clearly defined; possibilities for advancement are moderate, but predictable. After all, the prime motivating factor is not quick advancement, but doing one's assigned task thoroughly and reliably. There is little yearning for variety, since blue cultures set great store by routine and do not perceive it as drearily monotonous.

A position's place on the pay scale is just as fixed and transparent as the tasks associated with it. Special recognition or praise for individual performance is not, however, to be expected in blue culture. In fact, it would be perceived as embarrassing, such rewards being incompatible with blue modesty. What people in such cultures appreciate is the respectful recognition that they have fulfilled their duties. As for motivation by superiors, many blue organizations would agree with a proverb from Swabia, a German region home to many successful engineering companies: "No complaints is praise enough." Staff from other cultures or from abroad often find this hard to comprehend, being accustomed to good work being recognized and praised. But instead of a pat on the back and a "great job!," the best to be hoped for in blue cultures is a respectful nod.

Common standards

The effect of rules is not only limiting. They also simplify life. Standards reduce complexity and create predictability. International trade benefits vastly from the fact that a standard shipping container measures exactly 2.352 meters in width and 2.393 meters in height. Not because anything about these measurements was inherently superior to others, but because they form a standard adhered to by all. This makes loading infinitely simpler than having to play Tetris with containers, finding a fitting gap for differently shaped units. How irritating a lack of standardization can be is a commonplace experience: The variety of chargers for phones and laptops, for instance, not to speak of the international diversity of sockets to plug them into.

Standards are ubiquitous in blue organizations, be it in processes, procedures, and in forms—in HR, controlling, or production. The advantage is that standardization not just reduces the likelihood of mistakes, but also creates efficiency. As such, standards are a tested path to growth and the foundation for many a company's expansion.

Chain restaurants owe their success not least to blue memes. When Ray Kroc first visited a McDonald's in the 1950s, he was impressed by the rational efficiency of the processes he saw, reminiscent of Henry Ford's assembly lines. He persuaded the owners to let him join the business and expand it. He obsessively worked out the details of the restaurants he would open. Nothing was to be left to chance, least of all such pillars of standardization as quality, cleanliness, service, and price. McDonald's adheres to such principles to this day, as do many other food services and catering firms. Every guest is entitled to expect the same products in the same quality at every branch. Restaurants are furnished to uniform standards, and staff naturally wear uniforms, too. And indeed the Big Mac tastes the same, regardless of whether you order one in the United States,

Europe or Asia. Besides global standards, there are country-specific adaptations applying only to the appropriate division. In any case, however, a cook hoping to exercise his imagination and create burgers accordingly should look elsewhere for a job.

Unhealthy blue

Valuable though reliability and stability may be, there are also dark sides to blue company cultures. An excess of bureaucracy is one. Where everything that possibly can be regulated is regulated, organizations begin to resemble anonymous entities in which everything proceeds mechanically, but never dynamically, let alone pragmatically. When such a system becomes bloated, the resources needed for its upkeep are considerable. There is a price to controlling, regulating, and documenting everything.

Blue rules and regulations are also apt to create inefficiency where individuals might actually need the freedom to manage their own responsibilities and productivity. What is handed down from above as the right way of doing things cannot be adapted further down, because those charged with implementation lack both a view of the big picture and the right to make changes as they see fit.

Aiming for perfectly organized internal procedures, structures, and processes can be a trap for blue organizations for another reason: Internal affairs, not customers, are liable to be the focus of attention. What is going on in the environment, that is, outside the organization, is perceived as being of secondary importance.

Blue organizations tend to be stiff and rigid—that is the flipside of their reliability. What blue memes have devised is set in stone and above debate. This can lead to unhealthy dependencies. In blue cultures, everybody follows the rules—but what if they ought to be questioned? If they may once have been right, but the world has since changed? Blue rules all too often outlive their purpose. But instead of adapting them, blue memes expend energy on defending them at any cost.

Anything demanding a degree of flexibility tends to pose a challenge to blue organizations. Communication and the exchange of information may work along formalized channels, but not outside them, for instance, by situational, pragmatic networking. Job descriptions, by clearly spelling out the tasks to be fulfilled, implicitly define all the things that are *not* part of the job—and these things remain undone, as reliably as you would expect.

Doing one's duty thoroughly is one thing, to take the initiative oneself and create value even without a defined brief is quite another. In dyed-in-the-wool blue companies, people come to expect that "the organization" will stipulate targets and ensure development and coordination. To take things into one's own hand, assume responsibility, is seen as an absurd idea.

Blue's unforgiving attitude towards mistakes may produce reliable results, but stands in the way of experimentation. Blue companies are thus in danger of registering a rate of innovation as low as that of error.

Blue organizations run the risk of applying rules and structures developed at the head office to other divisions or subsidiaries, regardless of whether or not they are suited to local circumstances. A similar difficulty emerges when strongly blue corporations take over dynamic startups and subsequently impose their blue rules on them. In doing so, they suffocate the culture of speed and innovation they were hoping to benefit from.

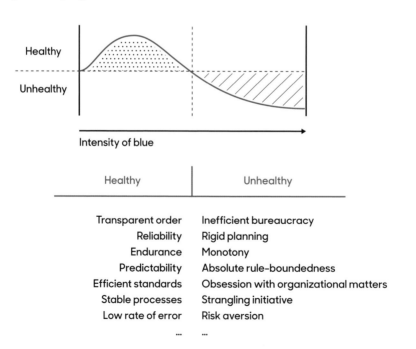

Healthy	Unhealthy
Transparent order	Inefficient bureaucracy
Reliability	Rigid planning
Endurance	Monotony
Predictability	Absolute rule-boundedness
Efficient standards	Obsession with organizational matters
Stable processes	Strangling initiative
Low rate of error	Risk aversion
...	...

Orange

From Tim's diary

November 17th

I can do it! If I can get MayCorp and Bell-Park Inc. to sign in the dotted line, I'll have met my sales target for the year—and earn $$$ in bonuses! ;-) And today I saw that Pete's not having a good month. At this rate, I'll have his parking spot right by the main entrance this time next year. Yeah! Anyhow, I really gave MayCorp and Bell-Park the works. MayCorp is going to pull some of next year's orders forward—for a discount, of course. They scratch my back, I'll scratch theirs.

And the company is generally doing pretty well, too. We're set to grow by 14 per cent this year. The Wave range is just what the customers want. And we're leading all the service rankings, deservedly, of course. WavePro is about to launch, and it's going to sell like hot cakes. What's more, we've done some pretty smart internal streamlining, and I expect there to be a fat bonus in it for me. In my performance review, I hinted that I could well imagine change of a further-reaching kind for myself. Seemed like a good idea to let them know where I'm at.

The only problem is Josh. He's just not delivering the kind of performance I expect. No initiative. No drive. No winning spirit! But for want of an alternative, I've got to hold on to him for the time being. But as soon as somebody better comes along, he'll have to go. I told HR to put out "discreet" feelers—don't want him to leave before we've got a replacement!

The coordinating effect of blue memes allows for stability and reliability. But even in the hierarchically ordered blue world, with its universally applicable rules, some people manage to live a better life and get into better positions than others. Even in the most rigid blue framework, they manage to find spaces they can use to their advantage.

As this realization spreads, acceptance of blue strictures begins to wane. Doubts over the many obligations and restrictions arise. The success of a few reveals there to be more than one version of the truth, and that there are ways to be master of one's own destiny. Instead of the one true path, orange memes indicate a variety of routes to success. The key is finding the most promising among them—without tearing down the system, which would be the red approach.

In orange cultures, the individual desires pushed to the back by blue memes stage their triumphant comeback. Infected by orange memes, people strive for success, advancement, and admiration. Everybody covets the top spot on the podium. People recognize that there are ways to improve their own lives. The key is seizing opportunity and finding the path to success. If they do, good work will find its reward, and much more 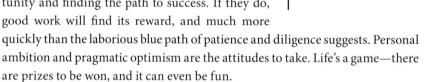 quickly than the laborious blue path of patience and diligence suggests. Personal ambition and pragmatic optimism are the attitudes to take. Life's a game—there are prizes to be won, and it can even be fun.

Historically, orange memes can be found asserting themselves whenever fresh starts are made, in the Renaissance for instance, or in the rebuilding efforts in Europe after the Second World War. The Declaration of Independence, too, contains distinctly orange ideas: the "unalienable rights" not just to "life," but especially to "liberty and the pursuit of happiness."

A founding father of orange economics was Adam Smith (1723–1790), whose work on *The Wealth of Nations* proclaimed self-interest and competition to be cornerstones of economic progress.[83] That competition produces losers as well as winners is to be accepted as a law of nature. "The winner takes it all, the loser's standing small," as ABBA put it. And there is always more to win. Orange ambition is never sated. "Greed is good", as Gordon Gekko, investment banker in the Hollywood classic *Wall Street*, put it.[84] And not just good: As far as he was concerned, greed is a crucial driver of human progress.

Competing to win

Though Gordon Gekko may have taken things a bit far, healthy orange memes are indeed an important motor in developing a business. In orange cultures, people take the initiative, identify opportunities, and look for solutions. Success is the key criterion in orange companies. Whereas blue memes direct the focus inward, on procedures, orange memes face outward, to where the game is played: toward customers and their wishes, the competition, and what's happening in the marketplace.

Scott Cook, CEO of the software firm Intuit, likes to explain that his company had the "47th mover advantage" on its side—not the first mover advantage.[85] At least 46 comparable products were already on the market, but in spite—or because—of them, Intuit saw an opportunity. While the competition's products weren't particularly user-friendly, Intuit found a way of pleasing consumers and soon became the market leader in personal financial software. The company stayed true to its commitment to strong customer service: The founder himself trained staff to identify problems users might have and to develop appropriate solutions.[86]

The Würth Group also displays obvious orange memes, many of which can be traced to its long-time head Reinhold Würth.[87] He turned a little hardware store into a global champion with 400 subsidiaries in 80 countries and a sales force of 30,000 employees. Würth's ambitious entrepreneurial spirit is solidly rooted in the company culture. One feature is that each leader spends several days a year working with the sales team. Numerous rankings make individual performance visible and comparable, thus promoting internal competition. Employees are set clear goals, in which the company's ambitious plans for growth are reflected. The pay scale is strongly performance related, and company cars reflect individual sales statistics. Further incentives are provided for finding and pragmatically implementing best practices: If it sounds promising, it's welcome here!

Bigger, better, stronger, faster

Orange cultures believe that improvement is always possible, that there are always opportunities to improve your life, and that "there's room at the top." All you need to do is to recognize your chances and seize them. As Richard Branson put it:[88] "Business opportunities are like buses, there's always another one coming." Not knowing what to make of an opportunity is no excuse, the Virgin founder is convinced: "Opportunity favors the bold! If somebody offers you an amazing opportunity but you are not sure you can do it, say yes—then learn how to do it later!"[89]

With all the opportunities before the mind's eye, and blessed with a healthy confidence in one's own abilities, orange dreams aim high: If Olympic gold or an Oscar are out of reach, then at least the equivalent in one's own field.

Talk of problems is unwelcome in orange cultures, which far prefer to speak of challenges containing opportunities. With confidence and drive, members look to make the best of any situation. Where others might be immobilized by negative thoughts, optimism prevails. And if something goes wrong? Never mind, hope dies last! Orange cultures are brilliant at constantly finding new motivation and making another attempt. Of course orange ambition doesn't enjoy defeat; but it accepts the inevitability of setbacks and firmly believes that other opportunities will arise.

Jeff Bezos leaves nothing about Amazon's culture to chance. Alongside the "relentless" red memes, he guides the retail giant with a good dose of orange: He demands that his employees display entrepreneurial spirit and performance orientation; he encourages competition and, above all, wants to see results. Amazon's leadership principles are full of orange memes:[90]

- *Customer obsession*: Leaders start with the customer and work backwards.
- *Ownership:* Leaders are owners. They never say "that's not my job."
- *Invent and simplify:* Leaders expect and require innovation and invention from their teams and always find ways to simplify. They are externally aware, look for new ideas from everywhere, and are not limited by "not invented here."
- *Hire and develop the best:* Leaders raise the performance bar with every hire and promotion.
- *Insist on highest standards:* Leaders have relentlessly high standards—many people may think these standards are unreasonably high. Leaders are continually raising the bar and driving their teams to deliver high quality products, services and processes.

- *Think big:* Thinking small is a self-fulfilling prophecy. Leaders create and communicate a bold direction that inspires results.
- *Bias for action:* Speed matters in business. Many decisions and actions are reversible and do not need extensive study. We value calculated risk taking.
- *Deliver results:* Leaders focus on the key inputs for their business and deliver them with the right quality and in a timely fashion. Despite setbacks, they rise to the occasion and never settle.

Amazon precisely evaluates and rewards individual performance. Top performers can look forward to handsome bonuses. Anyone wanting to take it easy is unlikely to be a good fit at Amazon: Staff tell of countless weekend and nighttime shifts, marathon meetings over Easter, and permanent availability when on vacation.[91]

Orange hunger for success keeps driving Amazon to explore new spheres in which to do business: The company's Kindle e-book-reader became the benchmark for digital reading, while Amazon diversified to sell nearly everything through a superior supply and delivery network. Amazon's video streaming service conquered a market one might have expected Blockbuster or TV networks to triumph in. Amazon's Cloud Service was considered a pioneer in the industry, again leaving established IT firms behind.

That some ideas, like the Fire Phone, should not fulfill expectations is part of orange entrepreneurship. To be sure, Jeff Bezos is no friend of failure. Yet he is convinced: "If you're going to take bold bets, they're going to be experiments. And if they're experiments you don't know ahead of time if they're going to work. Experiments are by their very nature prone to failure. But a few big successes compensate for dozens and dozens of things that didn't work."[92]

Orange cultures are acutely aware that every opportunity comes with a certain risk. They use tactics and cunning instead of the red bulldozer method. While red cultures live completely in the here and now, orange cultures have at least one eye on the foreseeable future. But results had better materialize by then, or else other, more promising opportunities will be sought out.

Entrepreneurial leadership

For leaders to be accepted in an orange culture, they must have one thing to show above all else: success. Standstill is the equivalent to a step backwards. The organization, too, must get better every year and above all outpace the competition. To this end, frequent use is made of targets and performance-related pay. The path to reaching a goal leaves room for autonomy and individual solutions, as long as the result is right in the end. Management by Objectives and Self-Control or Objectives and Key Results are leadership frameworks with crucial orange elements (see Chapter 4). Sam Walton, too, the founder of retail giant Walmart, follows an orange pattern in giving the following advice: "Set high goals, encourage competition, and then keep score." In an orange world, it's as simple as that.

Whereas red cultures use both stick and carrot, only the latter works in orange cultures. Staff are unlikely to stay long in an organization that threatens punishment. Instead, they are going to look around for an organization that offers more carrots.

Performance assessment is an essential orange leadership tool, because people want to know where they stand with respect to both the path to their goals as well as their performance in comparison to others. Only thus can they judge their own position and improve further. Like in sport, ratings make individual performance visible and act as a spur to competition. A former employer of mine asked new staff to take difficult written and spoken exams in their first months with the business. Results were published on the intranet. Internal pressure on performance was considerable—as were the novices' performances themselves.

Rainer Voss, once a successful investment banker and now retired, gave an insight into his trade's orange cultural patterns in the documentary movie *Masters of the Universe*.[93] His company's atmosphere was governed by ambitious goals like "10 per cent more every year—I don't care how you do it." Results alone counted. Whoever had the best knack for the game and knew the best moves could make his way in the bank—"no matter how old or how dumb you were," Voss notes. "You could become a celebrity in no time at all. I was very quickly promoted when I was young, and soon began to earn more and more money." That private life was to be subordinated to professional advancement went without saying. Anything else would have been at odds both with his own expectations and those of his peers. Alongside personal success, competition with rivals was a motivating factor, a thoroughly orange motive: "We had a clear rival, a competing bank. The stakes were implicit and known to all: We want to cut the deals the others have been making till now. And we want to do it better."

Practical experimentation

In general, orange cultures are open to new ideas; people are curious and eager to learn, especially if they expect knowledge and skills to help their personal advancement or reputation. Knowledge is interesting, as long as it helps in reaching goals. If half-knowledge will do the trick, they will settle for that.

Accordingly, two thoughts are the main drivers of curiosity in orange cultures: Is there an opportunity? And how can the desired results be achieved? The why is thus far less important than the how. A detailed grasp of all a problem's aspects is not even necessary. What is far more important is a pragmatic solution, which need not be theoretically watertight, but has to work in practice.

Orange cultures see change as a chance, not as a threat. For change means that the deck is reshuffled and everything is open again. Orange businesses know the market and their customers. They observe trends and scan the environment for opportunities. If an opportunity opens up, they will make a play for it, testing and experimenting. Just sketching ideas on a flipchart is definitely not enough. Experiments are crucial drivers along the orange way to innovation.

Silicon Valley startups have popularized the concept of "pivoting," which means rigorously dismissing a business model that has been shown not to work. It is orange cultural patterns that create such a resilient mentality capable of bouncing back from failure. It allows ambitious projects to be pursued with full commitment. But if, contrary to expectations, the bet fails to come off, the orange attitude is not to despair, but to brush off one's coat and try again. After all, Thomas Edison (1847-1931) was not put off by setbacks, but instead observed: "I have not failed. I've just found 10,000 ways that won't work."[94] As a canny inventor, he always looked for solutions that worked; as a canny businessman, he always had his customers in mind: "Anything that won't sell, I don't want to invent."[95]

Getting ahead pragmatically

Orange memes put pragmatism above principles, and quick wins over delayed gratifications. Orange positions are determined by a constantly updated cost-benefit-analysis. Orange entrepreneurial spirit sets priorities. What promises the greatest benefit is done; nobody would bother with something unpromising. To accord equal priority to a dozen projects would be anathema to orange sensibilities. You might as well pay everybody the same—unthinkable!

Contrary to the blue order, hierarchies and structures are handled pragmatically in orange organizations. Titles may be valuable for reasons of status, but the underlying structure is far less important. Communication thus occurs in all directions: top-down, bottom-up, but also horizontally and diagonally. Departments and individuals that might help in a particular situation are approached proactively. It is perfectly normal to skip rungs in the formal structure. Cooperation is sought with whoever is best suited to a given job, regardless of what an organigram may have to say about official divisions of tasks and responsibilities.

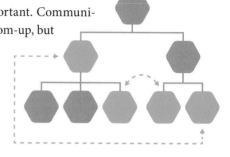

By and large, orange organizations are geared towards markets and sales. The organization is kept lean and supple, with bureaucracy reduced to a minimum. Bureaucracy, in this understanding, is defined as any process not quickly and efficiently yielding tangible results. What orange cultures want is autonomy and creative freedom, not constricting rules.

How goals are reached is neither here nor there. The end sanctifies the means, and hence, rules are interpreted generously. To the orange understanding, playing in a grey area is not breaking the rules. When Airbnb started to make inroads into what had previously been a fairly well-ordered hotel and accommodation trade, more and more competitors began to point out that the company was in breach of countless regulations. But Airbnb's self-image is not that of an unfair competitor, but as a smart broker and middleman, itself innocent of any wrongdoing.[96]

The pragmatism of orange decisions often transgresses boundaries clearly respected by others. Orange players have no qualms about interpreting agreements to their own advantage. Business partners are expected to understand that, in the interest of a better outcome, decisions may be made that contradict earlier agreements.

In strongly orange cultures, the competitive spirit is ubiquitous. It may thus occur that orange memes encourage the kind of behavior that others consider manipulative. From an orange perspective, however, there is no shame in wanting to influence people—after all, that's part of the game! It's about winning. Short-cuts are also popular. Steps or formalities may be cleverly omitted from a process. While others are waiting in line, orange players skillfully weave their way to the front.

As with all orange decisions, in conflicts the fundamental question applies: What good is all this going to do me personally in he foreseeable future? From an orange angle, taking conflicts out in the open is not always the smartest tactic. Discretion is seen as the better part of valor, at least if that seems the more prom-ising route. Such pragmatism may lapse into opportunism, and orange cultures run the risk of not just taking advantage of a fair wind, but of trimming their sails by it.

Looking after number one

From their first day of work, members of orange organizations have their career path firmly in view and pursue it ambitiously. In return, the orange organization judges them chiefly by their performance—the better it is, the higher the salary and the quicker the ascent of the career ladder. Relations with colleagues may have an important part to play, but only insofar as they help the individual's per-sonal or professional advancement. Cooperation is in pursuit of one's own goals; the individual ego is put on the back burner for as long as teamwork promises better personal outcomes than could have been achieved alone.

Anyone not up to the task, or unwilling to rise to it, is liable to be replaced by someone the organization considers more promising. McKinsey's Up or Out Policy is a generator of such orange memes. Every year, staff must face up to internal competition. Even long-serving partners are not exempted: Either they prove themselves, or they're out. The high fluctuation that such a system entails is accepted, for orange cultures seek dynamic progress, not stability. Results, not individuals, count—individual staff members are valued above all for the per-formance they deliver. Under the heading "Why I'm Leaving Goldman Sachs", a long-time employee of the investment bank criticized such attitudes and practices in an open letter:[97] "Today, if you make enough money for the firm (and are not currently an ax murderer) you will be promoted into a position of influence." Quite simple, really.

This high degree of competition and pressure to deliver inevitably leaves some by the wayside. But that is not to say that orange companies deliberately and systematically burn up staff. Instead, orange attention to opportunities can also lead to a form of talent management, in which people with the potential to achieve first-class results are selected and encouraged. Like a sports coach, an orange leader will pick its team based on performance. It is thus quite possible that a stalwart player is replaced by an up-and-coming one as soon as his form begins to decline. That's the nature of the game. Loyalty is not the strong suit of orange businesses, and its absence is mutual—staff feel no particular solidarity with their organization. If a competitor makes a better offer, they will not think twice about switching sides. "Better," in this scenario, refers not just to financial incentives, but to the entire spectrum of orange preferences, like room for career development, scope for action, status etc.

If you've got it, flaunt it

In an orange milieu, individual performance entitles one to recognition, respect, and admiration. It's nice to show off one's achievements: The top-of-the-range car, the exclusive designer dress, the desirable artwork, the special watch, the spacious office, the privileged parking spot—the orange world is full of status markers. Money is particularly useful because there is no limit to its accumulation: Imagine Scrooge McDuck bathing in his iconic Money Bin. Yet if you ask successful businessmen why they keep chasing after the best deals rather than retiring and taking life easy, the answer you often hear is that to them, money is simply a quantifiable measure of their success. In the words of Ray Kroc, the mastermind behind McDonald's:[98] "All money means to me is a pride in accomplishment." Beyond a certain point, then, money frequently serves merely as an orange indicator of success, as a quantifier that adds spice to the orange game.

Orange trophies are frequently material in nature, but not invariably so. Early on during my time in China, I marveled at the long nails taxi drivers proudly displayed on their pinky fingers. Inevitably, this is a status symbol: Peasants, by the very nature of their tough work, will never have long fingernails. The taxi driver is showing his world that he has made it. The same applies to the salesman of the month whose photograph is put on display. To be called onto the podium to be honored for good work at a company celebration is another orange motivator. It makes achievements visible to others.

In any case, orange memes make people measure themselves against their environment and to assess success in relation to competition—even where non-orange memes may not even be aware of a competitive situation: Of course the orange homeowner is fond of his exclusive residence—but only as long as it is the biggest house on the block.

Further indication of how widespread orange memes are is given by the following study:[99] People were given a choice between two hypothetical scenarios. In the first, they earned $90,000 a year, their neighbor $100,000. In the second scenario, candidates earned $110,000, that is, more than before, but their neighbor $200,000—far more than oneself. The results: The majority chose option 1. Relative wealth is more important than absolute. What counts is the ranking.

Unhealthy orange

An excess of orange memes causes people to become estranged from each other and their organization. In their exaggerated form, the competitive spirit and the desire constantly to outdo others take their toll on interpersonal relations. Cooperation and exchange in orange organizations occur not as a matter of course, but only if their usefulness to the individual is instantly apparent. There is only one thing to be relied on in an orange world: That everybody is out to optimize themselves.

"Bend the rules, don't break them," is another orange principle. Just how much give there is to the rules is a question that orange memes are likely to answer quite generously. This mentality renders moral scruples improbable, especially where "if everybody else is doing it, what's the problem?" is the dominant attitude.

"Sink or swim" is the rule, and even temporary underperformers do not last long in orange cultures. What is more, internal competition leads to valuable synergies within the organization being ignored, because there is a lack of coordination between self-optimizing units. The coordinating overall purpose of the organization is all too easily lost sight of.

Orange memes are largely unconcerned about the state of the business in ten years' time. Strong individualism and pragmatism in combination with a temporal orientation that is middle-term at best obstruct long-term, sustainable development. In a strongly orange culture, an expansive strategy process built around broad involvement, detailed ideas, and conscientious planning must seem too impractical and abstract; people would much rather try things out.

In general, orange is good at setting priorities. Yet this strength can conflict with another orange virtue, that of identifying opportunities at every turn. However many balls one may be juggling, from an orange perspective, there are always more opportunities waiting to be seized. There is a danger of getting lost in a world of unlimited opportunity and half-baked plans.

The more success people can lay claim to, the more recognition they receive in an orange world. But constant confirmation can turn healthy self-confidence into narcissism. The arrogance of winners spoiled by success can make their individual bonuses seem justified to them even if the business at large had a difficult year. Instead of rolling up their sleeves and mucking in, orange high performers are likely to leave sinking ships in order to fulfill their dreams elsewhere.

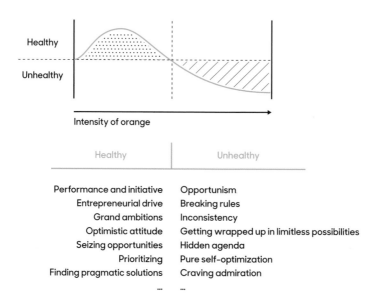

Healthy	Unhealthy
Performance and initiative	Opportunism
Entrepreneurial drive	Breaking rules
Grand ambitions	Inconsistency
Optimistic attitude	Getting wrapped up in limitless possibilities
Seizing opportunities	Hidden agenda
Prioritizing	Pure self-optimization
Finding pragmatic solutions	Craving admiration
...	...

Business Culture Design

Green

From Mark's diary

Wednesday, March 15th

Dear Diary,

Today was a good day! In our team meeting, we discussed our two troubled colleagues, Mary and Nick. We unanimously decided to have a development coach help them—the same we hired last year for Steve. The program really did Steve a lot of good; he's come a long way. I'm glad to see that, together, we were able to help him out of his slump. I think the whole team has benefited from that experience. Aside from that, in the meeting all of us in the team reflected on our conduct as leaders. Are we too strict? It's not easy being a leader. I hope that my team knows I'm always there for them.

I had lunch with Phil and Maggie. We took Maggie along to have a frank and open conversation with her. She's new with us and hence was extremely surprised by our feedback that her impersonal emails had ruffled some feathers. It wasn't easy for us to mention this, but I think it'll help her build better relations with her colleagues. After lunch, we went for a little walk together. Spring truly is in the air already—how wonderful!

In the afternoon, I prepared the performance reviews, which are taking place over the next few days. I need to be thorough, because I take these interviews very seriously. I'm really proud of my team and I want them to know it. I wonder what feedback they'll give me?

Just before leaving for home, I received an email from senior management containing the latest stats: 3 percent growth across the board, good news. Only the Springfield plant is still running at a loss. But we have made a clear commitment to keeping it running, come what may. There's no question of laying off people—after all, we take pride in putting people first.

In perfect harmony

Not just the world of business, but also technology, science, and the general advancement of humanity stand to benefit from a judicious dose of orange drive. Orange memes carry the potential to advance individual lives considerably, not least in their material aspect. But the price of success is often loneliness. For where only the idea of competition counts, there is little room for acceptance or true friendship. Yet the Beatles knew: All you need is love!

Once they have caught green memes, the winners of the orange race want not only to be envied, but also liked. And rather than being excluded, the losers want to be respected as part of the community. Instead of the rat race, they would prefer living together in perfect harmony. Instead of winning and keeping, the emphasis is on participation and sharing.

Unlike in the blue community and its impersonal order, green cultures try to approach people in a personal, sympathetic manner. And whereas in purple tribes, the relationship to a particular group or collective takes center stage, green cultures focus on the individual. Here, everybody is accepted. Every person is good, and his or her history, background, personality—all this is important, and all this is good. Green cultures are genuinely interested in people, their perceptions, and feelings.

In philosophy, an instance of green thinking may be found in the work of Jean Jacques Rousseau (1712–1788). Rousseau believed in the goodness of humankind, which had been corrupted by bad social institutions. The customs and mores of his age, too, he found to be worthy of criticism, seeing vanity and selfishness everywhere. His ideas were a strong influence on the French Revolution, whose motto "liberté, égalité, fraternité" can indeed be seen as transporting green values—even if the revolution itself, like all revolutions, was driven strongly by red memes.

The Romantic movement of the early 19th century also spread green memes: As a reaction against the orange-blue Industrial Revolution and purple-red aristocratic systems of government, the artists and poets of the era lauded nature and the peace people might find there. The hippies of the 1960s rallied to similar values. Their demands for peace, equality, and a non-authoritarian, anti-materialistic social order were aimed not just at red war, but also at the orange-blue establishment at large.

The people business

Writing about the waves of labor migrations from southern to northern Europe in the 1960s, the Swiss man of letters Max Frisch remarked: "We called for workers, and human beings answered."[100] Green companies are well prepared for this, treating their staff not as a workforce to be exploited, but as human beings to be respected. Starbucks, for instance, refers to its employees as partners and is proud to provide generous healthcare benefits even to part-time staff.[101] The company is committed to diversity and promotes integration and equality in all departments.[102]

Green memes of collegial affection create an atmosphere in which people need be afraid neither of their leaders nor of making mistakes. A multicolored heart is the logo of Southwest Airlines, the world's leading low-cost airline. Its mission statement contains green elements alongside more strictly commercial ones: "To become the World's Most Loved, Most Flown, and Most Profitable Airline." Among the values[103] impressed on staff are "be a passionate team player, treat others with respect, be egalitarian, follow the Golden Rule, put others first …".

Green memes foster deep trust in personal relationships. Staff feel that they are appreciated as human beings. In green cultures, people share a strong and mutual interest in perspectives, opinions, and concerns. Staff at Ubiquity Retirement and Savings are asked to press a button every day on leaving the office to indicate their mood.[104] There are five buttons to choose from, ranging from a very happy to a very sad face. The insurance company collects these data in order to get an idea of how their staff are doing.

New arrivals at green companies can expect to forge new contacts quickly and soon get to know all colleagues personally. It is quite common for executives to welcome new members of staff and lead them around the office, making introductions along the way. When new colleagues are introduced in the company magazine or intranet, at least as much space is given over to personal information as to professional qualifications or previous career stations. After all, interest in people extends beyond what they can do for the business.

In organizations, green memes create what is commonly called a "pleasant working atmosphere." Offices are not cold, impersonal workhouses, but comfortable and appealing, Office doors tend to be open, and executives have an open ear for concerns. A good work-life-balance is also valued highly. Excessive hours are unusual in green companies. Attending a son's soccer game or a daughter's birthday party rather than doing overtime is not usually an issue. In any case, there will usually be a colleague willing to hold the fort for the duration. And of course, green solidarity is assured anytime in case of sickness.

Even the weakest link of the chain can expect help in a green group. Nobody is left behind. That giving is better than receiving is everyday practice. Helping others is not a chore, but inherently motivating. People help each other gladly and like to feel needed. Green colleagues are friends.

Hierarchy and privileges have no place in friendships. On the contrary: To single out individuals would harm the structure of friendship. Preferential treatment is given not to those who stand out on account of their achievements, but to those in need of special support.

In a green community, all are of equal value, and hierarchies are flat. Even senior management doesn't insist on special parking spots, and doesn't mind standing in line with everybody else in the cafeteria. Profits are to be distributed on a fairly equitable basis, keeping pay differences relatively small. Fairness means that everybody receives more or less the same—and indeed more in cases of acute need. A friend of mine gave me an insight into his experience as entrepreneur and the green preferences of his business:

The most important thing to my staff is fairness! Nothing causes general upset so much as a few people feeling treated unjustly. Once, we made the mistake of rewarding the exceptional performance of a young and ambitious employee with the car of his dreams. We never heard the end of it! I never thought that would be such an issue. The thing is: If everybody has to take a cutback—no problem. But a few individuals receiving more? Big problem. I'm worried that this will lead to leveling-down and generally discourage people from excelling.

Big-hearted leadership

As a rule, the fluctuation rate in green companies is quite low. This is due not only to the good working climate, but also the centrality of close personal relationships. In green cultures, leaders act not so much as superiors, let alone stern drivers, than as coaches, supportively standing by their team members. The coach is part of the team, supporting all, just as team members are expected to help each other. Where other cultures give instructions or even commands, green leadership operates more by suggestions and consensual decisions. In a green culture it breaks a leader`s heart to dismiss somebody, or even bring less bad news. In cases of individual performance not living up to expectations, the leader will try to understand the employee's position, clear away obstacles, and redouble support. Development programs, trainings, or coachings are readily offered. There is a reluctance to blame employees for poor results or take them to task personally. To find fault with individuals runs counter to green team spirit.

The pillars of the green concept of leadership consist of what management books like to call "emotional intelligence." Daniel Goleman, that idea's most popular proponent, listed the following traits as being united in the emotionally intelligent leader:[105]

- *Self-awareness*: knowing one's own feelings, emotions, and motivations, and being able to understand their effect on others.
- *Self-regulation*: the ability to control one's own moods and impulses.
- *Empathy*: the ability to understand other people's emotions and address them appropriately.
- *Social skill*: the ability to build and cultivate relationships, to find a common denominator and build a consensus.
- *Motivation*: taking pleasure in work beyond money or status.

Praise is given generously in green companies, which believe that only happy employees perform well. But such recognition is not primarily for the benefit of individuals: much emphasis is placed on the collective achievements of all participants. For its own part, green management sets store by modesty. Etiquette demands hiding one's own light under a bushel rather than seeking public acclaim for successes. The green sense of community also suggests assigning responsibility collectively rather than to individuals.

Nobody in green cultures expects leaders to know all the answers. And showing weakness, far from undermining their authority, earns leaders respect. This, too, is a result of the personal relations between management and staff. Thinking about personal behavior, be it one's own or that of others, is common in green organizations. Feedback about oneself is welcome—preferably of course of the 360-degree kind, revealing a variety of perspectives.

Central green motivations for learning are an interest in people and in finding solutions collaboratively. Individual assessments or grades, on the other hand, are frowned on in green cultures. It is more important to develop a good sense of a situation than to be able rationally to penetrate into all its details. Accordingly, green senior management decides not on the basis of reports and data alone. Board members much prefer to visit branch offices and seek personal exchange with employees there.

Teamwork built on trust

Generally, green memes are important wherever people are concerned with their relationships and interactions. Without a generous helping of green, teamwork and mutual trust would be unthinkable.

Mention of green elements at Google is likely to evoke the image of an extravagant working environment, more like an adventure playground than a traditional office. Yet the leadership style at Google is not always as green as this fun image might suggest. The company's startup culture bore the imprint of its founder, Larry Page, an aggressively ambitious and analytically brilliant man. With his obsessive quest for knowledge and technological solutions, he was for many years the organization's driving force. Social skills, on the other hand, were not his strong suit. When Page returned as CEO after some years of intense personal development, he addressed his top executives in a remarkable speech:[106] Henceforth, he said, there would be "zero tolerance for fighting" at Google. He admitted that in the past, Google had expected a good deal of ruthless aggressiveness from its executives. That had only worked, Page continued, because the challenges Google faced at the time were linear in nature, for instance, taking the market share from nil to competitive to winning. Now that challenges were getting more and more complex, it was time for executives to learn to work together.

Google long operated on the assumption that to build the best teams, it was enough to bring together the smartest minds. It was time to put this assumption to the test.[107] Under the heading of Project Aristotle, hundreds of teams were scrutinized by statisticians, analysts, organizational psychologists, and sociologists. Had team members known each other before? Were their interests similar? How did incentives work? What was the balance between introverts and extroverts, men and women? Initial results were disheartening: "We looked at 180 teams from all over the company," reports Abeer Dubey, a manager at Google's People Analytics Division. "We had lots of data, but there was nothing showing that a mix of specific personality types or skills or backgrounds made any difference. The 'who' part of the equation didn't seem to matter." But it also appeared that something else had considerable bearing on a team's success: a culture of personal trust and mutual respect in which people can be themselves and rest assured that their contributions will not be rebuffed, ridiculed, or punished. In the best teams, members listened to each other and showed empathy for the needs and feelings of others. Project Aristotle showed that this also applies to an ambitious, data-driven organization like Google.

Responsibility as a brand

The green forte—building interpersonal relations—is useful to companies not just internally, but also in their external relations with customers or suppliers. Customers entering a restaurant or shop full of green memes will immediately feel that the friendliness with which they are received is sincere. In relations with suppliers, too, it is a good feeling to be able to rely completely on the other partner's fairness.

What is more, green companies feel an obligation towards society as a whole. Every effort is made to avoid harming other people or the environment. Maybe a listed premium fashion company seems an unlikely place for green memes to thrive. But the success story of Italian designer Brunello Cucinelli and his eponymous label is full of them. Cucinelli seems sincere in assuring his customers, staff, and shareholders that "money is valuable only when it is used to improve people's lives and development. And that is our aim."[108]

His company has committed itself to an exacting ethical code, which enshrines social responsibility, ecology, and human dignity. Staff, known at Cucinelli as "anime pensanti" (thinking souls), are paid 20 per cent above the market average, and management pay is capped at eight times that of an average worker. Cucinelli let it be known that his company would never squeeze customers or suppliers. While the business could not survive without making a profit, he maintains that "profit is not a value in and of itself. Profit must serve human dignity—or profit has no value."[109]

Meanwhile, the example of Götz W. Werner proves that green memes can thrive not only in the luxury segment, but also in mass-market retail with its focus on prices. The founder of the European drugstore chain dm is known for the resolutely anti-authoritarian leadership style he introduced throughout the company. He makes a point of preferring dialog to giving orders.[110] Staff involvement is extensive, ranging from work schedules to pay scales.[111] Every one of the company's 50,000 employees is to be valued as a person. As Werner emphasizes: "If we've made too big a profit at the end of year, we've done something wrong. It means we've invested too little—to little in our customers or too little in our staff."[112]

Sugar and spice and all things nice

Green cultures are egalitarian. Anything that might so much as hint at inequality is avoided. People making an effort to distinguish themselves strike the members of green communities as arrogant and presumptuous—and dangerous to the community. Political correctness is the green way of life. Every effort is made to avoid discriminating against others; nobody is to feel excluded. "Merry Christmas" conveys compliments of the season in a purple manner, whereas "happy holidays" reaches out to those of other faiths and none. Even small deviations from political correctness, in jokes or offhand remarks, give rise not to laughs, but earnest concern.

Communication is a core element of green cultures, preferably in personal conversations. Just as important as listening is reading between the lines and finding the hidden connections. Green empathy helps a real dialog to emerge. Time is not of the issue: Discussions last as long as it takes to present and understand all positions. Little wonder, then, that meetings in green organizations can be long and involved. Naturally, a great many people are invited—as far as possible, anybody who wants to participate or stands to be affected by the outcome. It is always considered preferable to discuss without reaching a decision than deciding something without it having first been duly discussed. Perhaps that is what the Bavarian humorist Karl Valentin had in mind when he observed: "Everything has by now been said, just not yet by everybody."[113]

Everybody who wants to can participate in a green decision-making process, regardless of position or experience. Consensus counts for more than cold, hard facts, anonymous studies, or abstract notions. As a rule, the opinion of friends or colleagues outweighs that of formal authorities or outside experts. Divergent opinions are registered, and decisions ultimately based on emotion rather than reason and logic. It may often take some time to get there, but once a compromise has been reached, it is binding for all.

If, however, conflicts should arise in a green team, its members are faced with a paradox. On the one hand, everybody has the right to be heard, and every opinion counts. On the other hand, differences of opinion disturb green harmony. For this reason, people are perfectly willing to put their own needs and desires on the back burner. Green memes do not permit standing one's ground. People will put on a cheerful face to keep the peace, but may inwardly be bitter and resentful. This green craving for harmony makes lingering conflicts or problems hard to recognize. For on the surface of things, everything is, as it were, "in the green." When dark clouds gathered at Lehman Brothers, a conflict-averse culture had already developed within the executive team. At the time of the crash, Lehman Brother was "one of Wall Street's most harmonious firms."[114] Nobody wanted it to disturb the peace by pointing out fundamental problems. As far as the board was concerned, critical debates were taboo.

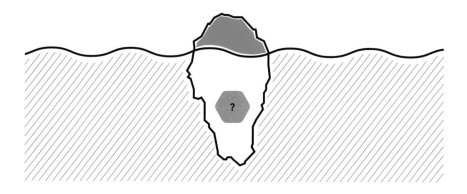

Unhealthy green

Tragically, unhealthy green often develops in companies when everything has been going well for quite a while. Coasting along and spoiled by fairly easy successes, they become prone to self-satisfaction and drifting off into complacency.

A culture insulated from harsh blows, in which the focus is on everybody's wellbeing, can be oblivious to changes in the outside world. But even when change is noticed, the organization is hampered by the time-consuming process of reaching a compromise. Finding a solution that satisfies all and puts nobody at a disadvantage takes time. If this process goes on for too long, even crucial decisions continue to be postponed and renegotiated until absolutely everybody concerned is on board. The craving for harmony in the here and now stands in the way of a genuinely critical discussion of the best solution. Crucial decisions are avoided if they are expected also to produce losers. Green organizations are profoundly averse to painful cuts, like shutting down an unprofitable branch or laying off staff, even if the entire company's viability depends on them.

Green conformity can suffocate any stirrings of individuality. Taking the initiative, stepping out of line, acting independently all run the risk of violating the principle of equality. An excess of community feeling in green organizations can thus undermine responsibility: Everybody relies on being helped out when in need. Instead of taking matters into their own hands, people in green cultures prefer to rely on others. Green teams are also liable to lapse into a collective "let's do everything jointly" mode; ultimately, nobody feels responsible for the outcome.

The friendly manner prevailing in green cultures can be hard to square with the professional demands of business relationships. Being on personal terms with customers, suppliers, or other stakeholders can prove a disadvantage when it comes to making difficult decisions. Personal relationships and feelings for people stand in the way of rational necessities. Green decisions follow the heart—the head is not always involved.

The green reaction to hostility is, invariably, green, which is to say discreetly reticent. But always turning the other cheek is apt to wear down even the most patient green culture, nor is it an effective long-term solution. Conversely, the most severe punishment in the green code, withdrawing friendship and affection, has little deterrent effect on aggressive opponents. As a consequence, the frustrated green community falls into self-pity rather than channeling its frustration into energies for change.

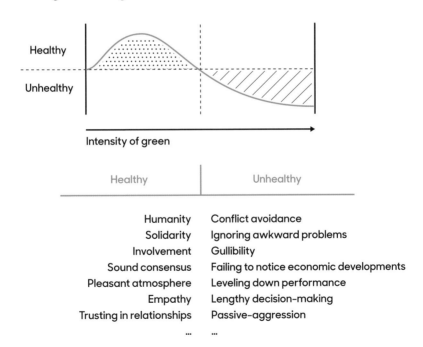

Healthy	Unhealthy
Humanity	Conflict avoidance
Solidarity	Ignoring awkward problems
Involvement	Gullibility
Sound consensus	Failing to notice economic developments
Pleasant atmosphere	Leveling down performance
Empathy	Lengthy decision-making
Trusting in relationships	Passive-aggression
...	...

Yellow

From Peter's diary

December 12th

On the whole, I still like it here at DataSi, even after 5 years. It's the longest I've ever stayed in a job! Sometimes, I think about the time at Epsilon, how boring and superficial it was. OK, the money was good, put the pressure to sell and the rigid procedures left me without the slightest bit of freedom. And then the expectation that one day, I would become a "real" member of the Epsilon family. But I never wanted that.

I'm clearly in a better place here. It sometimes reminds me of my university days, back in the lab—it's just as interesting and exciting. And I have my "Digital Diary" app to prove how much better things are going here than they did at Epsilon.

The algorithm for Sigma 12 is coming along brilliantly. That program is really amazing. Nobody else in the industry has anything like it. It gives us insights into product utilization of a kind we never had before. Terabytes of data are going to give us answers where we used to rely on our gut. That'll help us to automatically make better and faster decisions. Right on target! For Sigma 12, I collaborated with Janine from Singapore and Tom from Sydney via our X-Change app. I couldn't help noticing, once again, that Janine isn't the easiest to work with—but never mind. She's got the skills, which really helped us.

Project "Quest X" has been running for 2 weeks. I drew up the framework and am filling it in with data now. I've received all the info from our partners in Germany and England. The Dutch are still complaining that the whole concept is too theoretical. I don't get what their problem is. In the manual, we took 45 pages explaining its practical use. That really should be all anybody needs! Why don't they get it? I guess I'll have to send them the complete white paper with all the parameters ...

Green memes create a culture of humaneness and integration. In doing so, they undoubtedly make life more pleasant. But for all their sincere efforts, people will always find themselves faced with problems that no amount of sincere green inclusion and outreach will solve. Though it may be possible to keep on helping each other, wouldn't it be better to attack the problem by its root? To do so, however, the right knowledge is more important than good personal relationships. It is against this backdrop that yellow memes evolve, which seek knowledge, ask questions to find answers, and in doing so, hope to discover something altogether new.

"Sapere aude," dare to know, is the motto under which Immanuel Kant placed the Enlightenment. It is also the motto of yellow cultures. Rational knowledge is sought and followed. Yellow cultures obey the voice of reason, not their hearts or guts. In the age of Enlightenment, old ideas were challenged by new knowledge and ultimately disproved. Knowledge properly so called was based on curiosity, logic, reason, and scientific rationality. The great thinkers of the age wanted not to believe, but to *know*. Yellow cultures do not just find received opinions to be boring, they find them to be limiting. They aim to achieve freedom and clarity of thought. They are convinced that only an open mind can ask the questions that lead to truly illuminating answers. Only when prejudice and taboo have been put aside can true research and discovery begin.

"The illiterate of the 21st century," according to Alvin Toffler, the famed futurologist, "will not be those who cannot read and write, but those who cannot learn, unlearn and relearn."[115] Even the most radical of Enlightenment thinkers could not have dreamed of the sheer quantity of information that today, in the age of digitalization, is available to all. There are data sources wherever one looks. Now that a large number of people are already connected, information sharing is quickly expanding between non-humans as well. The "internet of things" is the shorthand for this seamless and automatic process of gathering, transmitting, and processing information. A car can communicate with a garage, a fridge with a phone, and a forklift truck with its freight. The information generated is rightly called Big Data. In yellow terms, you might call it Big Knowledge.

As early as the middle of the last century, leading management thinkers predicted that knowledge would become the crucial resource for businesses. The internet and digitalization have exponentially accelerated and intensified this development.

The fascination of the undiscovered

James Jorasch is the founder of New York's Science House—the kind of place where yellow memes thrive. When we met on the beautiful Italian island of Ischia, he was excited about showing off his new toy: an algorithm that analyzes all the most important chess matches of recent decades into their minutest details. To a passionate chess player like James, this was at least as mind-blowing as the beauties of the Amalfi Coast. He immersed himself in tables and statistics in order to develop a program to analyze future matches. "Why are you doing that?", I asked him. He answered: "Because I'm curious. I really want to know. Nobody has ever explored this before!"

These explorer memes are what drive yellow cultures and enable them to cast off familiar ways and completely rethink things. Neither their own experiences nor the expectations of others stand in the way of finding radically new ideas and solutions. What counts is the possible, at least in theory. Whether a discovery brings riches, meets with mass approval, or changes the world is of lesser importance. The fascination lies in discovering something hitherto unknown.

It was this fascination that, in the late 19th century, drove Gottlieb Daimler to a darkened garden shed near Stuttgart. With his friend Wilhelm Maybach, he spent all hours of the day and night hammering away—the noise even brought them to the attention of the police, who were curious what secrets the two hobbyists were keeping from the world. It was finally revealed in 1885, when Daimler's son first test-drove the wooden riding carriage. In fact, this contraption was the world's first automobile, powered by its first gasoline engines. The two brilliant inventors had devoted themselves absolutely to this progressive project: Their plan was not to improve the horse, but to create an entirely new means of transport, independent both of rails and muscle, of human and animal strength.

Gottlieb Daimler's technological skills, however, far exceeded his entrepreneurial ones. The financial fruits of his work were ultimately gathered by others, since he was loath to let himself be distracted by commercial considerations, as he wrote to a friend: "It really is the darnedest thing that [...] the technician's methodical thoughts are derailed by the brisk merchant."[116]

In strongly yellow organizations, curiosity is a discipline in its own right. Free-floating yellow thoughts allow creativity to develop. New ideas sparkle on all sides. Finding answers and solutions to challenging questions and problems is not just yellow cultures' strength—it is their passion! The associated tasks are performed with ambition, endurance, and thoroughness. Open-mindedness is combined with curiosity, long-term thinking, and the pleasure taken in being challenged intellectually. Ideas emerge from yellow organizations that to others may seem futuristic, often unrealistic, and at first sight incomprehensible.

Google is known as an incubator of yellow memes. Employees have reported that working there can feel like a never-ending thesis defense.[117] There is no shortage of smart people ready to place any idea under the closest intellectual scrutiny. Google's founder himself, Larry Page, finds the best connection with his staff to be via ideas and knowledge—not feelings. He is interested in his employees' individual skills and abilities. One of Google's most remarkable and successful initiatives was its so-called "20% time" policy. For many years, Google employees were encouraged to use 20% of their working time to pursue a project that interested them—one of the few stipulations was that it had to have something to do with the company's activities. The idea was to promote creativity and innovation. And indeed many products, like GoogleNews, AdSense, or Gmail, started life as such a project.

To ensure that the desired yellow mindsets were attracted in the recruiting process, Google applied yellow filters. For instance, the company placed an enormous billboard alongside a Silicon Valley highway displaying only a riddle:

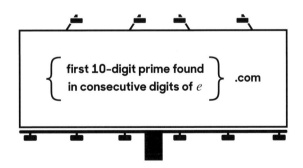

$$\left\{ \begin{array}{c} \text{first 10-digit prime found} \\ \text{in consecutive digits of } e \end{array} \right\} \text{.com}$$

The answer—7427466391.com—led to an anonymous website containing a further riddle. If that, too, was answered correctly, the reward was an invitation to send Google a résumé.

But yellow memes are in evidence not just among the tech industry's usual suspects. Even companies offering supposedly simple products and services seek a competitive edge from new knowledge. The electric toothbrush Oral-B Genius was, appropriately enough, launched at a major tech fair. It knows exactly how well which teeth have been brushed, and which ones are in need of closer attention. The built-in sensors provide users with feedback, helping their teeth to get as clean as possible. They also alert users if too little or too much pressure is being applied. A mobile app uses the phone's camera to take a photo of the user's teeth and create a personalized brushing plan. If you thought a toothbrush was a simple instrument, this system is designed to make you thing again.

However, the yellow thirst for knowledge is not limited to the product's application. It extends to production methods, storage and logistics, sourcing practices and more, all of which are precisely analyzed and evaluated. Data is gathered, combined, and interpreted.

Progress is good

A medium-sized company, Gerhardt Braun is the market leader in partition systems, specializing in basements and cellars. At first sight, it might seem that there is little scope for applying technological innovations in this sphere. But on the contrary! The company makes use of an earth observation satellite, which provides images and data for construction projects.[118] This service is provided by Building Radar, a young company from Munich, whose algorithm trawls the web for global construction projects of all kinds. "Spot projects 2–3 years before construction starts!" is the head start Building Radar promises its customers.[119] Perhaps, in a few years' time, every business involved in the construction industry will use such services—but those with yellow memes are sure to do so sooner.

In less yellow cultures, I often hear words to the effect of "progress is all very well, *but* …". There is no such "but" in truly yellow cultures, which agree that "progress is good." Period. Yellow organizations are passionate about this cause. They already had email accounts when everybody else was still hacking away at typewriters. And a little later on, they considered email a thing of the past and moved on to Slack and other communication tools. Yellow "technology evangelism"[120] is free of boundaries or taboos in its enthusiasm. To the yellow mind, there is barely anything today that might not be replaced by an algorithm before long.

In the sitcom *The Big Bang Theory*, the physicist Sheldon Cooper inhabits a world full of yellow memes alongside his friends: another physicist, an engineer, and an astrophysicist. True to the yellow pattern, Sheldon regards relationships as having the sole purpose of exchanging knowledge. All the social stuff with its customs and manners he could do without. His yellow matter-of-factness stands in the way of social connections. Yet he does try to form friendships, albeit in a distinctly yellow fashion: with the aid of an algorithm.[121] His attempt, however, does not meet with the desired success. The algorithm gets caught in a loop when trying to find shared interests. Those of Sheldon's opposite—horses, watersports, and rock-climbing—are not exactly the yellow hobbies likely to appeal to him.

Wired magazine calls the internet pioneer Marc Andreessen "the man who makes the future."[122] Andreessen likes to emphasize that digitalization and inter-connectedness will bring about a process of selection: "The spread of computers and the Internet will put jobs in two categories. People who tell computers what to do, and people who are told by computers what to do."[123] Yellow memes help cultures to be part of the former category. They are at the forefront of progress. They develop wherever people are intensely engaged with new ideas. *The Economist* was far from dismissive when it gave its cover story about Silicon Valley, the "brain of the tech world," the title "Empire of Geeks."[124]

Accordingly, "be nice to nerds. Chances are you'll end up working for one" is a piece of advice that took the internet by storm, where it has wrongly, but not altogether surprisingly, been attributed to Bill Gates. And indeed many of the companies that have grown massively over the last decades have done so by pushing their founders' yellow memes. It takes a good helping of yellow to get ahead in technological competition.

The knowledge economy

In yellow organizations, information is accessible to all. There are few secrets. To yellow minds, sharing knowledge does not mean giving it away and thus losing it, but rather multiplying it. Many observers were surprised when Elon Musk announced, in a blog entry on Tesla's website, that his company was not going to protect its patents.[125] Its knowledge was to be available to all, including the company's competitors. Patents, Musk explained, would only stand in the way of progress. Ultimately, not just other manufacturers of electric cars but also Tesla itself stood to profit from a shared technology platform.

Although the yellow mindset may be rather individualistic at heart, yellow cultures are fully aware of the huge advantages to be gained from experts forging connections. After all, the aim is to utilize the best knowledge, the best skills available. To this end, they reach out to their experts, forming networks of knowledge in which specialists can bring their skills to bear. Proven authorities in their fields are especially welcome. But yellow teamwork is not about people, it is about facts and solutions. The knowledge of others is more than welcome when needed. Yet it is also considered perfectly legitimate to withdraw into one's own private space to put one's thoughts in order.

From a yellow perspective, the world appears as a wealth of interconnected variables. Only if these are understood can the world be understood. Just going for the closest solution at hand will never do. After all, every supposed answer raises further questions, which, in turn, entail new answers and further questions. Though the quest for answers is far from easy, yellow explorers keep a level head. In such cultures, knowledge is not just the foundation of decisions, but also of morality, ethics, and principles. To draw the appropriate conclusions, things must be truly and fully understood. Problems are approached from all angles with an open, curious mind. Unlike orange knowledge, which is often content to make do with a superficial grasp of matters, the yellow thirst for knowledge strives to understand all there is to know with respect to a particular question. Digging deeper is a matter of principle for yellow memes.

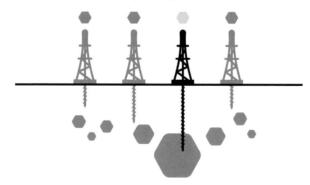

Answers are pursued with endurance and ambition, but barely has the first been found before yellow seekers become aware of the questions raised in turn. So they dig deeper for knowledge—and ever deeper. Yet the source of information is always an important consideration, for yellow cultures know that many misapprehensions are simply based on false information. This makes it all the more important to be in possession of the right sources of knowledge and generally to rely on facts, which is to say, as complete a set of data as possible. And the quest itself is pleasurable, though it may be lengthy and full of setbacks. Finding the answer makes all the efforts worthwhile and spurs yellow explorers on to keep up their research and bring yet more information to light.

Logical arguments

In their pursuit of truth, yellow cultures simply follow the laws of logic, which offer proof enough. After all, they were good enough for Albert Einstein, who deduced the existence of gravitation waves by mathematics alone. Only many years later could these curvatures in space-time be measured. By yellow standards of evidence, Einstein's perfect theory would have sufficed even without being confirmed by observation.

Elon Musk, too, is guided by the austere principles of science and logic.[126] He explains: "In established companies, managers think in analogies. They have no choice. Everything they do or don't do follows by analogy with previous experience. Institutions accrue institutional knowledge." This trove of experience is indispensable for the further development of existing products, as Musk is well aware: "Thinking in analogies is necessary to survival." But it is equally clear to him that "the electric engine must replace the internal combustion engine, because it uses energy more efficiently, loses less energy to warmth, responds and accelerates faster, requires less maintenance, creates more space inside the vehicle, can recover electrical energy when braking, does away with the need for expensive gearboxes, and emits fewer greenhouse gases into the atmosphere." It is by such compelling logic, not previous experience, that his enterprises should be guided.

Anyone taking an opposite view in yellow culture had better come prepared with compelling arguments. Yellow memes receive criticism neither with pangs of guilt nor aggressively, but as a rule with genuine interest. If the arguments turn out to be well considered and logical, adopting the new truth is no problem for yellow cultures. If, however, arguments turn out to be specious or distorted by emotion, they don't stand a chance. Something that makes no rational sense will never win yellow approval. The same is true for half-baked compromises or superficial consensus.

There are always several solutions to a problem, and yellow creativity is nearly boundless in identifying them. All possibilities, all lines of inquiry are conscientiously analyzed before the most rational solution is picked. Unlike orange tactical considerations with regard to the environment, yellow decisions are reached strategically. The objective is not to score a quick win, but to look well ahead into the future.

Yellow decisions are made based on knowledge and facts. The people consulted are experts in possession of relevant knowledge. Unlike in green cultures, it would not occur to anybody to ask everyone for their opinion. What use would that be? Yellow models and concepts for reaching decisions are as complete as possible—and hence extensive and complicated. After all, the flood of data, variables, and connections requires precise evaluation. It takes its time for all scenarios to be analyzed thoroughly enough to base a rational decision on them. This is not made any easier by the fact that though yellow opinions may be as profound and informed as is humanly possible, they are not by any means to be considered final. Opinions are prone to change in line with changed facts.

In yellow cultures, change is a normal fact of life. Considering that the environment is seen as a construct of interdependent dynamic variables, stability would even be something unnatural. Personal change, too, is easy for members of yellow cultures, for whom moving to the other end of the world for a better university education or a more exciting job is no big deal. On the contrary: Yellow memes cause people to go where things are the most interesting for them personally.

Free development

Yellow freedom means being oneself, and this tolerant attitude is extended to others.

Business Culture Design

There is simply no perceived need to adapt. Yellow cultures value diversity and particularly people who display traits that make them unique. Such peculiarities are considered far more interesting than collective conformity. Even if yellow tolerance does not set out to tell others how to live their lives, it is not always easy to get along with yellow ways. Their tolerance reaches its limit where other opinions cease to be rationally defensible. Then, the yellow attitude turns from approving acceptance to one of grudging toleration or open disinterest.

There is also an individualistic side to the yellow yearning for freedom. Submit to a clan, follow rules, or conform—never! Unhindered personal development is the goal, but not in order to gain recognition, power, or riches. In yellow cultures, people want to develop *as people* by accruing knowledge and thinking through big questions. With regard to material comforts, by contrast, the attitude tends to be rather minimalistic. A yellow student bedroom may be full of the latest IT gadgets, but will show little evidence of more than the bare minimum having been spent on clothes or food.

Organizing knowledge

"The Edge," an office building in Amsterdam, must be a yellow dream house. Thanks to innovative spatial and energy systems, 28,000 sensors, and a specially developed smartphone app, it deserves to be called one of the most intelligent office buildings in the world.[127] As such, "The Edge" represents a future in which people are connected with machines as well as each other by tracking systems that make the working day easier. Chock-full of new technology, it is the perfect yellow shell for knowledge organizations. As soon as a tenant enters the building, the elevator knows which floor he or she will want to go to—after all, every tenant, every employee, is electronically identified on arrival. The building communicates with the phone to coordinate its owners' working day: Depending on what the situation calls for, the app leads them to desks, conference rooms, meeting spaces, or rest areas. Lighting, heating, and even the coffee machine follow personal preferences—of course the machine knows who tends to take espresso or cappuccino and when. Even cleaners are told if any corridors or floors were in particularly heavy use during the previous day, or if others were hardly visited and no cleaning is likely to be required.[128]

Yellow knowledge organizations are structured around skills, not hierarchies or people. Tasks are assigned and undertaken according to knowledge and ability. Organizational structures, management systems, and regulations are accepted in yellow cultures, but only as long as they are perceived to be useful and make sense. Pointless bureaucracy, inflexible hierarchies, or unchanging habits are far less likely to meet with acceptance.

Little respect is accorded to a leader whose position is owed primarily to nepotism or questionable organizational structures. In yellow organizations, authority derives from knowledge and skills, not hierarchy, and is thus situational. There are specialists in each field, and hence the person with the most authority is the one who can contribute most to solving a problem. Diversity is valued not just for offering opportunities for individual development, but also to ensure optimum utilization of as wide a range of skills as possible.

One of the main challenges facing leaders in yellow cultures is keeping all their explorers on target. Focus and direction are easily lost sight of when there is much to discover, analyze, and understand.

Business leaders with a strong yellow tendency like to see themselves as playing the part of the conceptual mastermind. They lead by knowledge, wrapped in ingenious concepts. They like to develop strategic models, which, when filled with sufficient data, determine direction and decisions. Of their staff, they demand independent and responsible action. There is little point in expecting personal affection or sympathetic attempts at motivation from such leaders. Nor are they needed, for people in yellow cultures neither seek the limelight nor expect others to share their interests or preferences. They are intrinsically motivated and thus content to be left alone to tinker away at a promising idea, invention, or solution. Depending on the situation, they may do so in networks or entirely on their own, without an audience.

Staff loyalty towards the company depends very heavily on the yellow opportunities for development on offer. As long as there are interesting projects to which to devote their detailed attention, employees see no reason to change jobs. If, however, there is no scope for professional development, or if autonomy is too strongly curtailed, for instance by rigid standards, there is little to keep them in the company. Even higher pay, more free time, or the promise of rapid promotion would not sweeten the deal under such circumstances. For its part, the yellow company is hardly a paragon of solidarity either. If certain skills are no longer needed, yellow rationality suggests parting ways. What could be more logical?

Unhealthy yellow

"Nothing is more practical than a good theory!" is a thoroughly yellow creed. Nonetheless, an excess of yellow memes can hamper an organization and, in extreme cases, even paralyze it. Even the simplest things end up being made complicated, with the result that even inconsequential decisions are overanalyzed. Yellow memes fiercely latch onto a problem and look for solutions. If, however, the problem concerned really is the *critical* one is a question that yellow eyes can lose sight of. Their own interests override the organization's goals. Yellow experts have the stats on all their trees at their fingertips, but none of them has an overview of the forest as a whole.

In yellow cultures, interesting topics are attended to meticulously and with considerable endurance. Time is immaterial when yellow thoroughness is at stake.

The idea that sometimes the bold move is to accept a gap in knowledge is alien to them. Only other matters that are at least as interesting can distract yellow attention from the matter in hand. Strongly yellow cultures can thus get entangled in the details not just of one topic, but of several at a time. Yellow experts then come to resemble the cliché of the bumbling egghead.

A working atmosphere charged with yellow memes is not the most conducive to a team spirit emerging. Their autonomous attitude, geared towards the pursuit of personal interests, means that yellow experts prefer not to have limits imposed on their tinkering, be it by others or by structures. Generally speaking, they approach others dispassionately and with little emotion. They thus have difficulties inspiring other cultures and persuading them of their own ideas. Crammed as they are with facts and figures, yellow reports are not calculated to win hearts. Yellow ideas thus run the risk of remaining just that—ideas. Nor is rolling up one's sleeves to get involved in an idea's practical implementation the yellow way of doing things.

Reason can explain a great deal, but not everything, least of all when people are involved. Yellow notions come up against their limits when not clearly measurable aspects are at issue. The attempt to quantify them in order to feed them into yellow decision-making algorithms is doomed. All too often, then, the human factor is simply ignored.

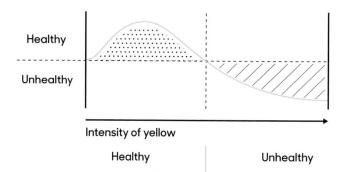

Healthy	Unhealthy
Spirit of discovery	Complicating simple issues
Taking pleasure in progress	Taking questions to extremes
Gathering and analysis of data	Getting bogged down in detail
Rational bases for decisions	Personal specializations before team spirit
Logical connections for guidance	Unemotional relationships
Focus on knowledge and skills	Theories lacking implementation
Critical questioning	Quantification even of soft factors
...	...

Business Culture Design

Aqua

From Mary's diary

January 12th

We really can make a difference! This once more became clear in our start-of-the-year meeting. Our vision is clear: Our *Panta Rhei* proposal has the potential to deliver superior comfort to our customers and save energy at the same time. If we succeed, we will create customer value while helping the environment. We may be there in four years' time!

A decisive factor is sure to be how well we succeed at integrating internal and external research, our suppliers, and the various production units. In order to do so, we will have to coordinate different organizations with completely different business models, cultures, and interests. It's a good thing that we cultivate such stable relationships with our partners.

Nobody minds that we still have a long way to go before we get there. We're all 100 per cent behind the mission and are wiling to make personal sacrifices if need be. Looking back, it's obvious how much our company has changed (once again) over the past few years. Not a trace left of *MillEx* thinking, though that was until quite recently our core product—the cornerstone, so to speak, of the company's identity.

The media are complaining that we're closing two of our European branch offices. Yet with a view to the future, it's quite inevitable. A perfectly normal process to secure our long-term viability. After all, what's at stake here is *Panta Rhei,* not individual sensitivities.

Peter, our colleague in finance, still needs to fully arrive here. He gets hung up on details and keeps trying to find structures. He seems troubled by the absence of superiors, an organizational plan, and fixed budgets. If he can't manage to adapt his controlling standards to our dynamic systems, I'm afraid we'll have to look for somebody else.

Panta rhei—everything flows

Yellow memes aspire to knowledge and personal freedom. In doing so, they often get lost in the depths of their own analysis. A great deal of energy is invested in exploring the individual trees. The forest, however, the big picture, remains unseen. Yet even the most exhaustive knowledge of a single part cannot explain the system as a whole. The aqua perspective is less interested in particular trees than in the viability of the forest. Pure aqua considers the forest as an ecosystem as well as the systems that influence it in turn. In doing so, unlike yellow logic, it does not insist on providing a rational explanation or scientific evidence for everything: Aqua memes accept and learn to live with the ineffability and unpredictability of events. Everything flows—*panta rhei*, in the words of the ancient Greek philosopher Heraclitus.

Like the previous colors presented on the right-hand side of the Culture Map, aqua, too, displays collectivist tendencies, placing the overarching system ahead of individual self-interest. Moreover, from the aqua perspective, this system is particularly large, referring not to individuals, one's own group, or the institution, but to the world as a whole. Aqua memes have no less an aim in mind than making the world a better place. Naturally, they cannot hope to do so alone, but only in partnership with others. To the aqua understanding, solutions must be every bit as holistic as the problems they address.

Historically, aqua memes are in evidence, for instance, in the life's work of Henry Dunant (1828–1919), whose efforts led the founding of the International Red Cross and the Geneva Convention. Having witnessed the horrors of the battlefield, the conviction grew in Dunant that only coordinated international action could alleviate the suffering caused by war. A joint effort was to change the system as a whole. Dunant created aqua circumstances under which green humanitarian help could develop. Similarly, the founding of the United Nations after the Second World War was an aqua milestone. Climate conferences, too, follow certain aqua memes: The universal challenge presented by global warming calls for collective measures.

A more recent project driven by aqua (and also yellow) memes is Wikipedia, which has become the default reference work for millions of internet users. Its 40 million articles were written not by instruction, for financial gain, or with individual reputation in mind, but because its authors wanted to share their knowledge with the world. The system is open and, to a large extent, self-organizing. Participants choose what topics to write on. They can begin or expand, but also edit and correct articles.

But aqua memes are found not just in the non-profit sector. In the world of business, too, their importance is growing. Orientation by purpose, the ability to change, and self-organization are qualities increasingly required of modern enterprises.

Finding meaning and doing good

Viktor Frankl realized that humans are creatures in search of meaning[129]—for instance by doing something for the benefit of others, for the world. To endow one's actions with meaning is characteristic of aqua. Though other color clusters may do likewise—purple by contributing to the group, red in the struggle for freedom, green by benevolence, and yellow in expanding knowledge—no other value system is as intensely preoccupied with the meaningfulness of its own actions as aqua is. In cases of pure aqua, these actions must furthermore conform to the highest moral standards.

Companies in a variety of fields frame their mission using aqua elements to create meaning. They testify less to the companies' ambitions for growth and profit than to their wish to make the world a better place in a particular way. Just to give a few examples:[130]

Google: Organize the world's information, and make it universally accessible and useful.
Hilti: Building a better future.
Huawei: Building a better connected world.
LinkedIn: Connect the world's professionals to make them more productive and successful.
Sony: To inspire and fulfill your curiosity
Starbucks: To inspire and nurture the human spirit – one person, one cup and one neighborhood at a time.

In a strongly aqua environment, personal career development, power, or status are of interest not to bolster one's own ego, but only insofar as they help individuals to contribute to the greater good. Aqua memes lead companies not to look primarily for profit or market share, but to act in such a way as to give something back to the world by their actions. Sustainability and social responsibility are important values. To optimize oneself or the organization at the expense of others, by contrast, is not an option.

The success of Ben & Jerry's, the ice cream maker, contains a good dose of aqua memes.[131] Its products are made entirely of natural ingredients and according to high ecological standards. Ben & Jerry's was the first ice cream producer to source all its ingredients from suppliers certified as Fair Trade, from sugar and cocoa to vanilla and bananas.[132] Founded and built up in Vermont, the company continues to operate, maintaining its standards, as part of the ecosystem of Unilever, the Anglo-Dutch conglomerate.

Aqua convictions can also be found underpinning the success of The Body Shop, which produces and retails personal care products. The Body Shop took responsibility very seriously at a time when most of the cosmetics industry was still committed to animal testing. Products use all-natural raw materials only. Anita Roddick, its founder, made sure her passionate personal commitment to social justice and ecology carried over to the company. Her social conscience became a guiding principle. She was convinced that her customers were interested not just in looking after themselves, but also in helping create a world free of animal testing, exploitation, and ecological ruin.[133]

Salesforce.com, too, quite deliberately makes aqua statements. The company is known not just for its software and platform solutions, but also for its *Pledge 1%* scheme.[134] This pledge is founded on the so-called 1/1/1 model: The company makes one per cent of its products available free of charge to non-profit-organizations, and one per cent of equity is donated to community projects. Finally, one percent of working time is given over to charitable purposes: Each employee has seven paid working days a year to devote to a good cause. Not just Salesforce.com believes this to be a valuable contribution to making the world a better place: Other companies have since adopted this scheme.[135]

An organic perspective

The aqua meme filter perceives the world as a single great ecosystem. All its elements are in flux—hence, change is entirely natural. While yellow cultures seek to understand the world as a network of variables, through the aqua lens, it appears to consist of mutually influencing organic systems. The boundaries between these systems are permeable and fluid.

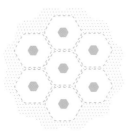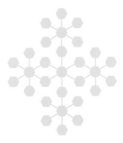

The aqua view of organisms is by no means limited to biological systems like humans, animals, or plants. From this perspective, organizations, departments, or teams are also living organisms. You may notice that the view of organizations as organisms outlined in Chapter 2 also corresponds to an aqua perspective.

In contradistinction to an analytic approach, which breaks down the whole into its component parts, what is at issue here is the nature of the whole. As Peter Senge, one of MIT's most iconic scientists, observed: "Dividing an elephant in half does not produce two small elephants."[136] The characteristics of living systems result from their wholeness.

Clear aqua elements are discernible in the central building of the BMW plant in Leipzig, designed by Zaha Hadid. Aside from its organic appearance, one of the celebrated architect's hallmarks, the building also displays functional elements that are clearly aqua. It was designed as the "nerve center" of the huge production site.[137] Its architecture is supposed to overcome the traditional divisions between departments and enable it to function as a whole. The *Architectural Review* has described the building as "a modern chimera—part showcase, part offices, part laboratory, part canteen."[138] Its fluid architecture connects the factory floor with offices, blue-collar workers with white, products with processes; it makes people aware of what is happening all around them. The conveyor belts that move car bodies from one section to another spectacularly wind their way along the ceiling of the central building—the nerve center—over open office spaces and even through the cafeteria. The vehicles constantly gliding overhead are a persuasive reminder of the common purpose to which all individual efforts contribute.

From an aqua perspective, the organism of one's own company is part of a vital ecosystem. In their striving to take advantage of collaborative synergies, aqua memes make companies less hesitant about reaching out to other organizations. No matter whether they are suppliers, subcontractors, research institutions, schools, production partners, or even supposed competitors: The aqua ecosystem is capable of integrating the most diverse spheres. In this respect, Toyota was a pioneer. The principle of "growing together with suppliers" has been in place since the company's early days.[139] As early as the 1940s, procurement policy was to consider suppliers' workshops as one's own and not to change them without sufficient reason. Suppliers were not to be squeezed or played out against one another, but given the opportunity to develop in tandem and share in the fruits of joint success. At the same time, Toyota made sure to work with more than one supplier at a time, in order minimize the risk of bottlenecks or quality issues. Consequently, Toyota's reputation with its suppliers was that of a tough and demanding customer, yet one who was also fair and reliable. The corporation thus, over decades, built up an ecosystem of its own. Where others cultivated an "us vs. them" mentality, Toyota strove to create a win-win situation for all involved.

Aqua memes see the individual, too, as part of the whole—but not as part of the purple clan, the blue institution, or the green community, but holistically, as part of the world. From this perspective, the significance accorded to the individual is not particularly great. A powerful government may use aqua arguments with little concern for individual anguish, for instance if communities require resettlement before building a dam that stands to benefit the system as a whole in the future. By the same token, senior management will not hesitate to close down a division if a long-term benefit for the company's viability at large is to be expected.

Individuals are but tiny parts of the universe, and of fairly small significance taken by themselves. This aqua view not only promotes modesty and humility. It also gives rise to the insight that great things can be accomplished only by working with others—using collective intelligence and making a joint effort.

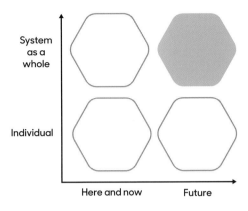

Like everything in the aqua world, relations within the company are in flux. Aqua memes create loyalty with a particular purpose in mind, but not necessarily towards the company itself. And just as a company must and may change, the same is expected of its employees. Anyone discovering a meaningful task elsewhere is to be congratulated, not kept at any cost. Far from cultivating jealousy or resentment at losing an employee to the competition, aqua memes encourage businesses to build up alumni networks to keep former members of staff within their ecosystems.

Orchestrating strengths

Each of the colors discussed so far has strengths that can be helpful. Aqua memes ensure that these individual parts are harmoniously orchestrated to form a symphony.

What millions of moviegoers love about the productions by Pixar is owed not least to aqua memes. Edwin Catmull, the studio's CEO, regards it as a key task of senior management to ensure balance.[140] Yet balance, as he understands that, is far from stillness. Like when balancing on a surfboard, the task is constantly to ensure the equilibrium of different, opposing forces. Producing a successful film requires a diversity of perspectives to be integrated, belonging to interest groups whose priorities may be partly at odds with each other: Directors want to tell moving stories; production designers want the images to be as visually impressive as possible; finance wants to ensure that everybody keeps to the budget; marketing wants a story that will sell; and merchandising looks for characters that will look good as toys or on t-shirts. Each of these groups is under pressure, looking to achieve something great, and, to that end, will fight for what it thinks is right. At the beginning of a project, in particular, there is often little understanding of how one's own priorities might affect the other groups as well as the overall outcome. "If any one of those groups 'wins,' we lose," observes Edwin Catmull.[141] A single group's success, in other words, comes at the cost of the whole. Catmull thus sees his task as creating the right balance: "In an unhealthy culture, each group believes that if their objectives trump the goals of the other groups, the company will be better off. In a healthy culture, all constituencies recognize the importance of balancing competing desires—they want to be heard, but they don't have to win."[142]

Integrating opposites

Like Yin and Yang in Chinese philosophy, aqua memes treat apparent contradictions as complementary and interdependent. The whole only emerges from the interplay of various forces. Whereas other value systems push strongly in one direction or seek compromise, the aim here is for a balance in which supposed contradictions support each other.

Alignment and autonomy are often taken to be opposite ends of a scale—a shared orientation at one pole, the freedom of self-determination at the other. More of one thus inevitably means less of the other.

Not so at Spotify,[143] which aspires to "aligned autonomy" and refuses to see a contradiction in this goal. On the one hand, the streaming service appreciates the motivation and quick decision-making that autonomy entails. Yet on the other hand, the company knows that it can be successful only if the autonomous teams all pull together, hence are "aligned". For Spotify, then, "aligned autonomy" means that leaders must concentrate on identifying the problems in need of being solved, and then task the teams with looking for possible solutions. This is doubly typical of aqua: Seeming contradictions are integrated, and leaders do not predetermine answers, but design a system in which solutions can be developed.

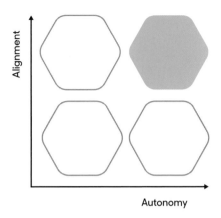

Spotify compares its version of the aqua symphony to a jazz band, in which all musicians play their own instruments and act autonomously. Yet they all listen to each other. After all, each musician is invested in making the song sound great. From the aqua perspective, the integration of different forces stands in the foreground. Strengths and weaknesses are recognized, controlled, and combined. Red impulsiveness and resolve are just as valued as blue reliability and endurance. What is more, an attempt is made not to leave green humaneness and yellow rationality to chance, but purposely to cultivate them where appropriate. Nor are orange initiatives and purple identity a question of either/or, but reveal the true well only in a healthy combination. Functioning in such a manner, aqua memes are system coordinators, which, with the big picture in mind, deliberately piece together patterns that are helpful in contributing to the company's viability.

Self-organization by fluid structures

To aqua memes, the world is a global brain, a huge biotope of multi-disciplinary knowledge and an infinite diversity of ideas. Intuition and spirituality have just as much of a place in it as do logic and rationality; guidance from scientific research is just as welcome as is gut instinct. There is great potential in this complexity. The individual components are systematically combined to form a greater whole. The challenge is not to know everything in detail, but to accept that gaps are inevitable and concentrate on the overarching patterns that emerge.

Since, to the aqua mind, every organization is an organism, it must be controlled accordingly: not by top-down instructions, but through a network of autonomous, self-organizing units. The aqua principle of self-organization has a good deal in common with the way the human body works: The plethora of information and functions in our system could never be controlled by a single organ. If the brain started micromanaging, the entire system would soon collapse. Each unit, be it a cell or an organ, processes information, produces output, and organizes itself while fulfilling its function. White blood cells, for instance, are free to react and produce antibodies as they see fit—no need to ask permission from HQ.[144]

In organizations, aqua memes promote fluid units instead of rigid structures. Small units can come together for a particular purpose and part ways once it has been fulfilled. Hierarchies and positions, too, are not set in stone. Teams form situation by situation, with no firm boundaries. Leadership emerges from each particular constellation. Seniority within the firm is of as little consequence as somebody's position on the career ladder.

Inspired by a comparison of cultures using the Culture Map, a Connected Culture Club formed at BMW. It brings together colleagues from different departments and levels of hierarchy to discuss matters of corporate culture. They exchange knowledge in order to make a conscious effort to shape their company's culture. None of them is obliged to do so, but all invest their own (unpaid) time in the Culture Club. Doing something for the benefit of the organization as a whole is motivation enough. Nor does the irrelevance of hierarchy lead to chaos. On the contrary: it helps the Club integrate contributions from a diversity of perspectives and develop creative solutions.

At the plastics manufacturer W.L. Gore, which owes its success in the fast-moving world of fashion to its innovative Gore-Tex technology, there are no hierarchies, no titles, no bosses. Employees are supposed to lead themselves.[145] "Rigid structures need to give way to self-regulating systems that form the core of an unfolding, 'fluid' corporate structure," explains Heinrich Flik, long-time managing director of Gore's German subsidiary.[146] Instead, Gore relies on dynamic networks, which are designed to encourage direct communication and increase the company's productivity and innovativeness. Anybody organizing a project will not fall back on his "own" staff, as defined hierarchically, but instead look for allies within the network. In place of superiors, Gore has instituted "sponsors" (similar to mentors) and "leaders." Employees choose their own sponsors, and even leaders are elected by the teams themselves—by virtue of their specific skills and their standing within the team. Such relations need not last long: A team leader for one project may well be a colleague among others in the next.

Heinrich Flik compares Gore's scheme with an amoeba, a single-cell organism capable of constantly changing shape. Though its outward form is variable, the amoeba's inner anatomy is remarkably simple and stable in structure. Such shape-shifting is not unusual at Gore, either. A unit may grow, require more space, and push aside another, which is then compelled to reorganize itself. Once a plant reaches a particular size, a new branch forms, like a cell dividing.

Responsiveness, that is, the capacity for reaction and adaptation, is an important principle in aqua organizational models. The organization reacts organically, and adaptations, too, occur automatically. Aqua memes bestow these abilities on Zara, the fashion retailer.[147] Traditionally, the clothing industry's collections change according to a fixed seasonal rhythm. Designers create collections and store managers place orders according to their experience of the previous season and their expectations for the next. The manufacturers then produce accordingly. Not so at Zara, where aqua responsiveness is coupled with red speed and yellow data. Consumers' purchasing decisions are constantly being monitored and analyzed. As soon as a trend becomes apparent, the information goes straight to Zara's design center. Designers are authorized immediately to carry out redesigns and pass them straight on to production, which in turn can react with a minimum of delay. Only a short time later, the new garment can be found on the racks. The precondition for such quick responsiveness is an holistic aqua perspective and coordination on Zara's part, which allows even orange-Blue considerations of efficiencies to be overridden: factories do not usually operate at full capacity, which allows them to react flexibly whenever new information demands adaptation.

From an aqua perspective, it is the nature of the business that a company must always be prepared to make changes. After all, it is to develop in a healthy manner and in line with its environment's requirements. Imagine setting sail across the Atlantic: It would not occur to anybody to set the rudder only at the beginning of the journey. To reach the destination safely, adjustments constantly need to be made—some light, some rather stronger.

Unhealthy aqua

Like no other color, aqua succeeds in mastering complexity. Yet, like all others on the Culture Map, this color, too, cannot succeed alone. Even the best conductor will be of no use as long as there is no orchestra to be conducted. Aqua memes fully come into their own when there are other cultural patterns to coordinate. They turn unhealthy when they lose sight of the other colors' uses or even start considering them inferior. Such a dismissive view harms the organization organism, for purple community-mindedness, red resolve, blue structure, orange ambition, green humaneness, and yellow curiosity can all be indispensable factors in ensuring viability.

Aqua memes find complex solutions to complex problems. Yet they tend to apply this habit to less complex challenges, too. In the everyday life of business, however, there are many matters that can be decided quickly and with little trouble—without taking into consideration all conceivable aspects and consequences.

Where everything flows, there is little stability and reliability. In its attempt to do justice to the world's dynamics, aqua control eschews simplified models for orientation like blue project plans and their mono-causal relationships, clearly circumscribed steps, and extrapolated assumptions. As a consequence, aqua solutions often seem vague and unspecific. This may accurately reflect the complexity of the situation, but does little to cast light on it. Nor is the constant striving for balance conducive to finding quick answers and pragmatic solutions.

Aqua control focuses on long-term, holistic work *on* the system rather than *in* the system. Direct intervention is avoided; the system is meant to organize itself. There is thus as little room in the aqua picture for people's everyday worries as there is for operative problems or short-term goals. Focusing on a future vision can often mean losing sight of the here and now.

Where altruism and spirituality get out of hand, the economic performance of the entire company is endangered. There is no point to the noblest visions if the means to make it come true are exhausted along the way.

Finally, the open aqua system offers little identification with the company, but rather with an overarching purpose. Though employees may derive meaning from a vision, the organization offers little security or sense of being at home—both values dear to many people.

Business Culture Design

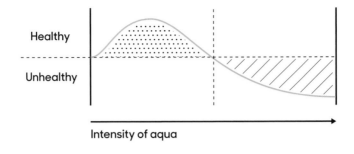

Intensity of aqua

Healthy	Unhealthy
Pursuit of selfless ends	Getting lost in complexity
Creating meaning	Utopian visions
Holistic perspective	Vague and unspecific solutions
Reconciling opposites	Underestimating real-life problems
Fluid adaptation to the environment	Excess of altruism and spirituality
Organization through self-organization	Awkward way of doing things
...	...

Hexagon perspectives

You have now been introduced to all of the Culture Map's seven colors. The following charts are designed to help you recapitulate the traits associated with each color and to recognize the differences.

Hexagon overview

Cultural evolution gave rise to specific memes as reactions to particular challenges. In response to these challenges, they developed their specific opinions and convictions.

	Challenge	Solution	Motto	Meaning found it	Heroes	Truth is …
	Danger	Joining forces with others	Strength in unity	Contributing to the common good	The most experienced	… what the leader says and the group believes.
	Submission	Dominating others	The world is a jungle.	Self-assertion	The strongest	… whatever prevails..
	Chaos	Creating stability	A place for everything, everything in its place.	Fulfilling one's duty	The most enduring	… what the rules say.
	Predetermination	Being master of one's own destiny	The winner takes it all.	Personal success	The most successful	… whatever gets you ahead.
	Inequality	Practicing humaneness	All people are good at heart.	Helping others	The kindest	… whatever contributes to harmony.
	Incomprehension	Exploring in order to understand	Sapere aude!	Knowledge	The smartest	… what can be proved.
	Complexity	Jointly addressing the big questions	Everything flows	Contributing to a better world	Those who make the world a better place	… as changing as the environment.

Business Culture Design

Mutual perceptions

You may remember Chapter 2: We see the world not as it is, but as we are. Seen through its appropriate meme filter, one hexagon is likely to have a particular view of other cultures. This overview shows what culture A may think of culture B, but rarely dares to say aloud.

	B	B	B	B	B	B	B
A	Completely normal	A danger to our community's stability	No sense of informal rules and norms	Unsteady, always chasing new goals	Naïve trust in strangers	Unbelieving sticklers for evidence	Make everything complicated
A	Dependent on others	Completely normal	Trapped by rules	Opportunistic	Wimps	Nerds	Dreamers
A	Nepotism	Anarchists	Completely normal	Cheater	Don't sanction misconduct	Ignore standards	Abstract
A	Live in the past	Obstinately impulsive	Insist on doing everything by the book	Completely normal	Hippies	Theoreticians	Altruists
A	Intolerant of strangers	Brutal	Impersonal	Materialist showoffs	Completely normal	Lone wolves	Oblivious to human dimension
A	Refuse to look ahead	Act before they think	Stifled by formalities	Confuse superficial with genuine knowledge	Sentimentality	Completely normal	No attention to detail
A	Blinkered	Short-sighted	Rigid	Selfish	Counterproductive desire for harmony	Detail-obsessed analysts	Completely normal

Decision-making

"It's important to make the right decisions"—and none of the seven perspectives would disagree. On how such decisions come about and who ultimately decides, however, ideas vary widely.

	How are decisions reached?	Who decides?
	Paternalistically, based on experience	The chieftain
	Impulsive, based on gut feeling	Whoever wields the greatest power
	In an absolutist style, strictly by the book	Whoever is authorized to decide
	Tactically, depending on what might work	Whoever is responsible for the outcome
	Consensually, all are involved	People jointly
	Fact-based, according to knowledge and logic	Data
	Holistically; not either/or, but looking for synthesis	The system designers

Getting there

Once the decision has been made, the hexagons are ready to go. Their memes determine how they set about reaching their destination.

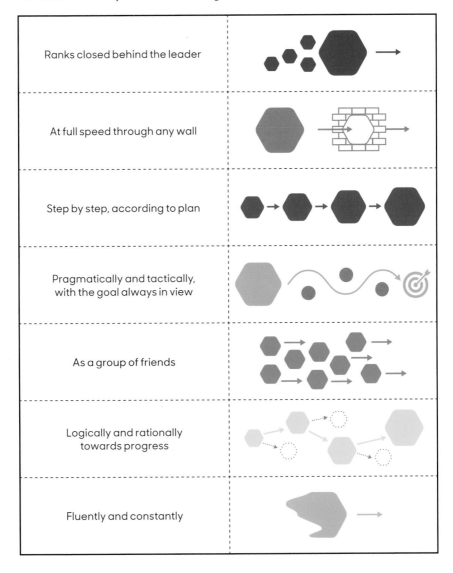

Ranks closed behind the leader	
At full speed through any wall	
Step by step, according to plan	
Pragmatically and tactically, with the goal always in view	
As a group of friends	
Logically and rationally towards progress	
Fluently and constantly	

Timeframes

The hexagons also differ in the temporal references and horizons that influence their actions and decisions.

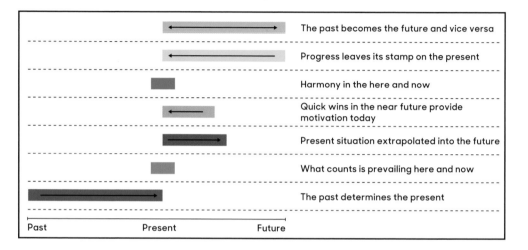

	The past becomes the future and vice versa
	Progress leaves its stamp on the present
	Harmony in the here and now
	Quick wins in the near future provide motivation today
	Present situation extrapolated into the future
	What counts is prevailing here and now
	The past determines the present

Past   Present   Future

Chapter 4
Corporate Culture Management

The Culture Map Initiative

Now you have been introduced to each of the Culture Map's seven colors, and maybe you will have found yourself nodding in agreement at some of the memes described in the previous chapter, recognizing them as part of your own culture. But as I have emphasized already: It is the combination of individual colors in a pattern that describes a culture—and by making it visible, it can be molded, developed, and changed.

There are four steps by which the Culture Map can help initiate a conscious and deliberate development of corporate culture:

1. *Culture check:* understanding the prevailing cultural pattern.
2. *Context check:* identifying the challenges a culture is facing and the opportunities open to it.
3. *Culture target:* giving cultural development a direction.
4. *Culture control:* the means by which you control a culture's development.

This is where things begin to look colorful! If you like, why not keep seven crayons in the colors of the Culture Map handy? The framework for Business Culture Design depicted here will lead you through the four steps listed above. Before you begin, define the "system in focus": Which culture do you want to analyze? That of the entire company? Of a department? Of a particular team? As soon as you have decided at what level the analysis is to take place, you can begin with the culture check. You can also use this framework in workshops in order to work out a cultural pattern with your colleagues. This has the advantage of letting everybody

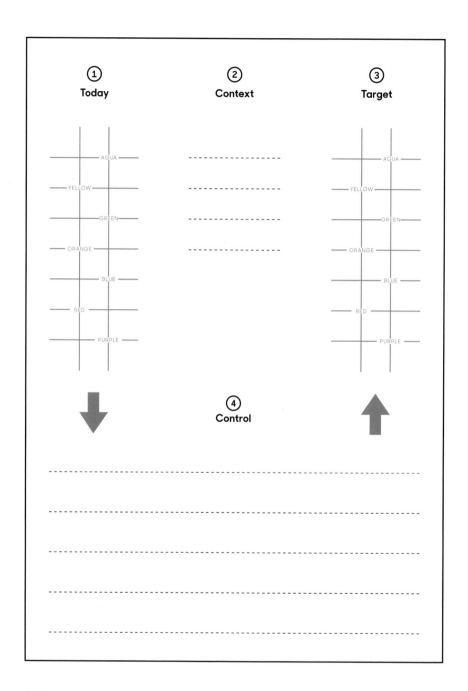

Internal perspective

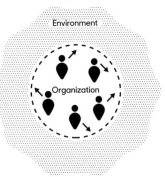

External perspective

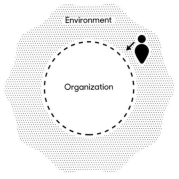

Internal perspective

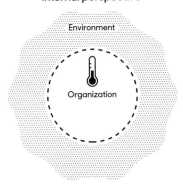

involved experience at first hand that "corporate culture" is not some fancy but ultimately empty concept, but instead is visible, tangible, and thus can be shaped. By jointly reflecting on culture, all are put in a position to understand and appreciate the target. The measures taken to get there will gain approval. The people involved in this way turn into active Business Culture Designers.

Step 1: culture check

The crucial question to ask yourself in this first step is: What mindset, what spirit, drives your organization today? Or to put it another way: Which memes control behavior? The answers will guide you in drawing up the Culture Map for your culture as you find it today. The stronger the effect of a particular meme within your culture, the larger the hexagon you should draw for it.

For the resulting picture to be of maximum validity, it is advisable to combine three perspectives: the internal view, the view from outside, and the results of a survey. When analyzing a culture, it is worth remembering that the complete picture can be seen neither from the inside nor the outside alone. Nor can culture simply be measured. The best possible picture emerges only from conscientiously combining the three angles.

- *Internal perspective:* Think—alone or jointly with your team—about how dominant the individual colors of your culture are. Experience shows that, when drawing up the Culture Map, it is easiest to begin by drawing the two largest and the two smallest hexagons. This quickly produces an initial rough draft of a cultural pattern, which you can subsequently adjust and complete.

- *External perspective:* As you know, we perceive the world not as it is but as we are. This self-image can be deceptive, because your culture is likely to have successfully infected you with its dominant memes. An external observer will judge your culture from a different angle. What seems normal to you may seem remarkable to an outsider—for better or for worse. The external perspective may be provided by stakeholders outside the organization, such as customers, suppliers, other departments, consultants, or even employees who are still new to the firm.
- *Survey:* Data gathered in a survey can help to reflect and, if needed, adjust an image that otherwise would be purely qualitative. A useful template might be the short questionnaire in Chapter 1.

Do the findings from these three perspectives agree? If, for instance, you ticked "mostly agree" for a color of which you have only drawn a small hexagon, this should encourage you to think again thoroughly about that color's importance. But please also be sure not to take everything the questionnaire might seem to suggest at face value. A quantifiable survey is only one means of obtaining information—not the only one. The same applies to outside feedback and your own experience. Every angle, however, helps you validate and sharpen the image of your cultural pattern.

By conscientiously performing the culture check, you will automatically be confronted with your culture's strengths and weaknesses—an important point of departure for any effort to develop your organization. A large blue hexagon, for example, signals order and reliability. If sizeable purple and green hexagons are also in evidence, there is reason to suppose that the culture will remain stable even in choppy waters. Yet if the hexagons on the left side of your Culture Map turn out to be rather smaller, you would do well to ask yourself how flexible and dynamic the company really is.

Step 2: context check

Developing a culture is not an occasion for wishful thinking. Culture is supposed to help the organism stay fit—that is to say, viable—in an ever-changing environment. Only if context is considered is it possible to tell what a culture's strengths are really worth and how much its weaknesses stand in its way. A glance at the organizational organism will provide orientation. The key questions in taking this step are: Which challenges must a cultural pattern meet? Where are opportunities to be seen?

If you are considering your culture at the company level, the decisive factors are most likely to be changes in the environment, such as market trends, customer needs, or technological developments. Beside these factors, internal challenges, for example a reorganization, a new strategy, or the staffing of key positions, are elements of the cultural context.

If the organization under consideration is not the business as a whole, but a department or a team, you should above all analyze the environment within the organization in which the department or team is embedded. In this case, it may be the company itself that makes the principal demands that the organism must live up to.

Step 3: target culture

The results of steps 1 and 2 will help you now to develop an idea of the culture you want to aim for—your target culture. In order to do so, draw a new Culture Map that represents your desired cultural pattern. But remember: There is no such thing as a *single* true and universally valid cultural pattern, one that is appropriate to every situation! There is a multitude of possibilities, depending on where the culture is coming from and what the culture wants or is supposed to deliver.

There are three categories that will help you decide which cultural traits to expand and which ones to reduce: Think about which memes you can use to which ends, which ones you absolutely need to change, and which ones you can continue to live with.

"Don't fight forces, use them" is an insight we owe to Buckminster Fuller (1895–1983), the visionary architect, systems theorist, and inventor. Business Culture Design should abide by this motto wherever possible: The task is to use a culture's existing strengths. But even a superficially harmful cultural pattern can often conceal helpful memes. Behind green avoidance of conflict, we often find empathy and tolerance. Patience and endurance can be cloaked in blue bureaucracy. And red aggressiveness tends not to be lacking in courage and resolve, either. These are useful qualities if used wisely and where appropriate.

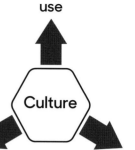

If you discover patterns that are not strengths in disguise and that weaken or obstruct the organism, you have two options: Either you change the pattern or you learn to live with it. This last may come as a surprise—after all, isn't the point to develop the best culture possible? But in the complex field of organization, it can make sense to turn a blind eye here and there, specifically when the benefits of attempting change are out-weighed by harmful side effects. A purple-green garden party may not be the obvious complement to the orange-red strategy your company has just decided on. But would matters really be helped by cancelling the traditional festivities and risking the resentment and resistance doing so would entail? The ancient Chinese strategist Sun Tzu (ca. 500 BCE) taught that not all battles need to be fought—which means that you don't have to declare war on each and on every meme that looks out of place.

Business Culture Design ought to concentrate on developments that influence a culture decisively. These need to be identified and shaped. The fields that actu-ally make the difference between success and failure are the ones that deserve your full attention. Perhaps you will have to break with a few venerable traditions throughout the company, but there are quite a few things that you can stick to without jeopardizing the organization's wellbeing.

If you develop a picture of your target culture not on your own, but together with your team, this step will reap a further benefit in terms of conscious Busi-ness Culture Design: You will have jointly agreed on the direction in which to take the development of your culture. In addition to strategic goals, like "improve quality" or "develop new products," you will have a beacon guiding cultural development. For example, everybody knows: "Next year, our focus is on orange and aqua. Departures from the purple-blue status quo are strongly encouraged." People are thus able to orient themselves towards a jointly devel-oped target culture.

Step 4: culture control

Once everybody is committed to the target culture, the question arises of how to add the desired memes to the culture. At this point, I am sure to disappoint anyone who expects this chapter to provide a list of mechanical controls by which to calibrate each hexagon. As I explained in Chapter 2, organizations are not machines, and it follows that people who work to develop cultures are not mechanics, but rather comparable to landscape gardeners (see Chapter 2). But this is far from suggesting that there is nothing you can do.

The best access to controlling the existing meme sets is by thinking *what* it is that controls behavior within the culture under consideration. Behavior that becomes habitual sooner or later develops into a culture. This happens automatically, with no further input required. Yet a culture's development can proactively be steered along a particular path. To this end, the following questions may help: Where do the dominant memes come from? What seems to amplify or reinforce these memes? Which new, alternative sources of memes should you consider to support cultural development?

To get closer to the heart of the matter, I like to use a simple psychological formula:

$$B = P * S$$

A person's behavior (B) is the product of its personality (P) and the surroundings (S). Both variables contain points with which cultural development can operate. P comprises an individual's motivations (*wanting to*) and abilities (*being able to*).[148] S contains social demands (*being supposed to*) and social consent (*being allowed to*)—the surroundings' expectations and incentives—as well as the situational context in which a person happens to move.

$$B = \overset{\frown}{P * S}$$

As the transmission of memes suggests (see Chapter 2), these two variables influence each other: people have an effect on their surroundings, and the surroundings are sure sooner or later to influence the people within it.

- *Variable S:* Where the surroundings promote and reward old behaviors, there is little chance of new behaviors emerging. New behaviors can be encouraged only by changing certain surrounding factors. All too often, leadership seminars or workshops close on a virtually elated note of confidence in the bold new steps about to be undertaken. But back in the office the next morning, everybody is back in their familiar environment—and resolutions are quietly abandoned one by one. After all, the path of least resistance is to fall back into line with one's environment: leaders, colleagues, and not least the numerous management systems that guide the organization's behavior, like targets, pay scales, career paths, performance assessments, procedural rules, and so forth. These factors in a person's surroundings exert a strong influence on which memes proliferate. They may reward red courage, blue punctiliousness, or yellow creativity. Depending on their cultural orientation, they may point towards any of the seven hexagons. Depending, however, on which cultural traits are to be promoted, they can also be adapted.

- *Variable P:* There is little point in trying to change somebody's personality just by reasoning with them, let alone by threats. More promising are measures aimed at personnel development, like additional qualifications, coaching, or mentoring. Especially if they enable new experiences and ensure that ingrained habits are questioned, they can help people to accept new memes. A targeted exchange of experiences, conscious reflection, or external feedback can contribute to illuminate an existing set of memes critically. Anything that enables a person to adopt a new perspective and come to new realizations influences that person's perceptions, thoughts, feelings, and, ultimately, actions.

  If a person is unable or unwilling to develop, variable P allows for another option: P can be changed by substituting the person altogether, i.e. finding someone new for the job. Naturally, a new person will contribute a new personality to the culture. It goes without saying that this effective method harbors great dangers and should not be taken lightly. Not only does a culture lose knowledge and abilities by substituting people, it is also in the nature of the organization's organism that individual components cannot simply be replaced as they can in a machine. It is more like a transplant. There is no guarantee for the new person being accepted by the organism. Personnel changes entail irruptions into complex social systems, leading to side effects in often unexpected places. Nonetheless, it may be necessary to think about reassigning or restaffing positions if a broader cultural change is to be instituted. The impact of individuals on a culture is too important to ignore their reciprocal effects.

And with this, we have come full circle, for personnel decisions also affect the variable S. An essential factor in a person's surroundings is simply other people—especially leaders. They are a powerful source of memes. Their daily leadership transmits strong signals about what kind of behavior is rewarded and promoted in the company's culture. A leader may praise, ignore, or mock red-yellow attempts to think outside the box. He or she may equally well initiate or suppress the exchange of green memes. Whether a leader chooses to interpret corporate guidelines in a conscientiously blue or a pragmatically orange manner also has a considerable impact on culture. As obvious as it may sound: Cultures are crucially shaped top-down, by the example leaders give. Somebody who makes a point of setting a particular kind of example, demonstrating, demanding, and valuing a particular kind of behavior, will end up infecting others with these memes. What is more, a culture's staffing decisions also demonstrate the kind of behavior considered appropriate and rewarded within a company, whether, for instance, orange emphasis on success or purple conformity is more likely to get someone promoted.

How radical Business Culture Design needs to be depends on a culture's fitness. It is much like personal health. To ignore your own body over a long stretch of time can come at a terrible cost. Though a heart bypass may save a life, it is not to be taken lightly, but instead still associated with considerable risks. Looking after yourself, on the other hand, and going for regular checkups, means reducing the likelihood of ever needing such drastic surgery. The same applies to managing a culture: Leaving a culture's development to chance means risking one day being in a situation in which radical measures are required to preserve the organism's viability.

Business Culture Design in practice

To better familiarize you with using the Culture Map, I have selected some anonymized cases from my practice as a consultant. To safeguard confidentiality, I have rendered the cases unrecognizable and given false names to the companies concerned. The following case studies show examples of how Business Culture Design works in practice.

A Culture Map workshop at an investment bank

The situation: MoneyPowerMoney, MPM for short, is a successful US investment bank with offices around the world. The team at the Hong Kong branch was looking to strengthen its culture. To this end, a Culture Map workshop was organized, in which the branch's entire senior management took part. The managers came from a wide variety of countries. Some had only been with MPM for a few months, and barely anyone for more than a few years.

Culture Check

In the first step, participants were invited to reflect on their culture as they found it at the Hong Kong office. Taking the Culture Map in hand, they discussed their prevailing cultural pattern and the strengths and weaknesses it entailed.

The Culture Map helped make the culture's strengths and weaknesses visible. On the one hand, MPM's ambition, determination, and flexibility were impressive. The company took its cues from the market and was quick to innovate. Yet it became equally apparent that short-term orientation jeopardized the company's long-term success, for its best hands soon left if the big bonuses didn't keep on coming.

Generally, this strongly individualistic cultural pattern exhibited little cohesion. The analysis barely revealed any collective values: no purple sense of community, blue structures, green relationships, or an aqua vision.

Though MPM has a long history to look back on, purple values barely have any part to play. Rather than being a true community, the company is a place where people come together to pursue their individual goals. These people hardly identify with the organization or what it stands for. There is a high employee turnover at MPM. People come and go, they are effectively mercenaries. It would seem absurd to them to regard the company as a family, much as the traditions in which other banks take pride seem absurd to them.

People expect their performance to be directly rewarded. They work hard to this end. What counts for them is the result at the day's or week's end—not some remote outcome at the end of the year.

They are restless and always on the lookout, ever ready to make decisions and to implement them right away. Markets change rapidly, leaving no time for doubt or hesitation.

Working at MPM is not for the faint-hearted. Conflicts are carried out openly and frank exchanges of opinion are the norm. Individuals are expected to tolerate a great deal of strain. Those who prevail quickly ascend the career ladder. Those who can't are never seen again.

Though of course MPM is not without formal rules and structures, they are not taken too seriously. Perseverance and patience are not the order of the day here—except in battling bureaucracy!

There is transparency with regard to formal hierarchies, career paths, and pay options. But these rules function more as motivators for ambitious staff than as a framework providing structure and stability.

MPM works towards success—day by day. Competition comes not just from outside—internal competition, too, is considerable.

People are ambitious in reaching their goals. They will make great efforts to gain money and status. In doing so, they are pragmatic and flexible. Short cuts are welcome, and everyone knows how to maneuver through grey areas. To bend the rules is not seen as breaking them—it's just the smart thing to do. Staff belong to the organization because doing so promises them benefits. If more is to be had elsewhere, they're off in the blink of an eye.

New opportunities—meaning potential profits—are quickly recognized and successfully seized. The staff at MPM are keen to show off their trophies in their spare time. They adore fast cars, expensive watches, and partying in the city's most exclusive clubs.

People at MPM say that they get on quite well together. But that's about it. They work together and celebrate their successes. But the wind blowing down the corridors is an individualistic one, with no hint of green empathy. Everyone looks after themselves. There is no expectation for anyone to hold back for somebody else's benefit. There are barely any deep friendships. To confide in somebody, especially personal pain, would be seen as a sign of weakness.

Everybody at MPM knows that feelings have no place in business. Actually, they appreciate the fact that business success comes first.

The world of finance is far from trivial. Numbers are decisive for success. The right analyses, models, and concepts make all the difference. These fields are where people at MPM feel at home. They are always in search of new knowledge—not general knowledge, but knowledge in their area of specialization: figures, stats, and facts to feed their analyses, models, and concepts.

People at MPM set great store by independence. Many strive for financial independence at a young age. Diversity is not seen as a potential obstacle. There is no expectation for people to have particular values or follow certain preferences. What matters are the skills they bring to the firm.

Developments in the distant future or the big picture are not present in MPM's collective mindset. The consequences of one's own actions, too, play a part only inasmuch as they affect short-term success. Instead of a vision or a common purpose, people are driven only by pecuniary incentives. Any kind of altruism, let alone wanting to make the world a better place, is out of place here.

Though MPM, too, donates considerable sums of money to charity, this is driven by orange memes. After all, even these donations are expected to deliver some kind of payoff to the firm, for instance in the form of good PR.

Context check

The context check identified drivers that pose challenges on the culture. The decisive factors were:

- *Tough competition in the financial services industry:* New fintech companies entered the market, offering radically different solutions.
- *Technological changes:* Technological cycles kept getting shorter. To miss one step meant falling behind.
- *Implementing the company's overall strategy:* The strategic guidelines set by the head office in the US had to be implemented in Asia, too.
- *Finding and keeping good staff:* Potential hires have come to expect more than just a good salary and other monetary incentives. A family-friendly lifestyle and meaningful tasks gained importance.

Target culture

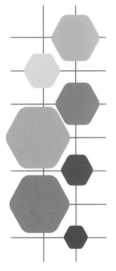

Important patterns in the existing culture were up to the demands of the future and were thus to remain in use: red speed and resolve as much as yellow enthusiasm for technology and orange competitiveness. The small proportion of blue memes was discussed, but ultimately not regarded as a major problem. By common agreement, it was something the office could live with. At the same time, while still in the workshop, managers came up with some ideas for how better to balance the culture. The aim was to stabilize the system by bolstering the collective side, especially by consciously activating purple, green, and aqua memes.

Culture control

Based on the culture check, the context check, and the target culture, specific measures were developed in order to actively shape MPM's culture.

The managers decided to strengthen the company's sense of identity and belonging at the Hong Kong office. Departmental information sessions were immediately to be replaced with town hall meetings, in which all would participate. This strengthened not only the sense of community, but also awareness of the company's overall strategy.

At the same time, employer branding was strengthened: Being part of MPM was to signify status and recognition, much like membership of an exclusive club.

Based on the overall corporate strategy, an ambitious joint mission for competing in the south-east Asian market was developed, which was to provide orientation for individual contributions. Subsequently, among other measures, individual remuneration was more strongly tied to the company's long-term development.

In future, managers were to be appraised on the basis not just of monetary criteria, but also on how they led and developed their staff. Leadership conduct was optimized by supportive measures such as personal coaching. Moreover, the company resolved to pay more attention to work-life balance.

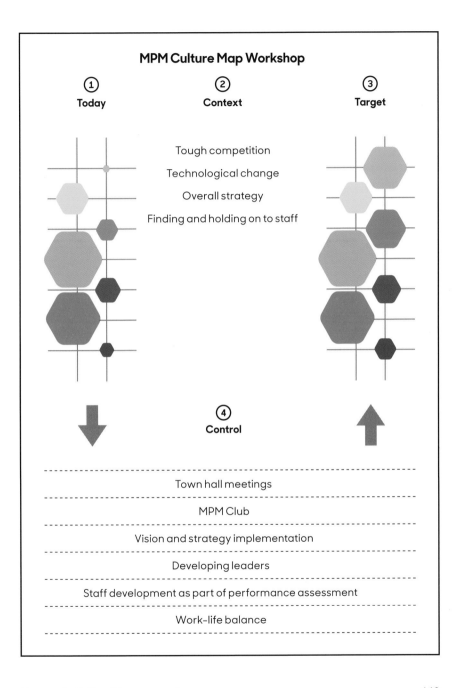

Post-merger integration at Maschinenbau Inc.

The situation: Maschinenbau Inc. is a mechanical engineering company based in southern Germany. Internationally successful for generations, Maschinenbau made its name with the superior quality of its products and the high degree of its processes' reliability. Customers could always rely on these standards being upheld. In order to stay at the cutting edge, Maschinenbau acquired Gyrosta, a young and innovative Swedish company.

A Culture Map analysis was carried out with the aim of supporting post-merger integration. Answers were sought to the following questions:

- What mindsets drive each company?
- What image does each company have of itself and of the other?
- What would be the cultural consequences of complete integration?
- What needs to be taken into account, from a cultural perspective, during integration?

Cultural & mechanical engineering

Maschinenbau was proud of its long and successful history. A family business for three generations, it now employed nearly 5000 people, with two thirds working at the firm's original seat and the remainder at branches in the US and China.

Purple values provided the company's culture with a solid foundation. Staff were proud to be part of the firm. The fluctuation rate was low; having parents or even grandparents who had worked for Maschinenbau was far from unusual. In the difficult years following 2008, mutual support and communal spirit became especially apparent. The company and its staff moved even closer together in order to weather the crisis jointly.

As the main contributing factor to its enduring success, Maschinenbau cites the continual improvement of quality and productivity. Its culture is molded by strong blue memes. The organization functioned much like the machines it produced: in a structured, precise, and reliable way. Nothing was left to chance; everything was standardized and dealt with transparently. Leadership was built around organizational charts and job descriptions. People were highly conscientious in carrying out their tasks, working with great care, thoroughness, and endurance.

Maschinenbau's blue and purple pattern was also shot through with red memes. From the owner to the line manager, leadership was by authority and clear orders. Team efforts were rewarded rather than contributions from star players. Leadership would tolerate no deviation from blue rules or purple habits.

A healthy if modest dose of green values helped Maschinenbau to foster a working climate that was broadly perceived as agreeable. Orange, yellow, and aqua memes, on the other hand, were less in evidence. A look at the previous years' success brought this into sharp relief: It was founded on the continual improvement of traditional products, that is to say, on incremental innovation. Maschinenbau was far from making the quantum leap towards new products.

And indeed the company's culture showed virtually no evidence of the orange drive to uncover new opportunities or find pragmatic solutions that might conflict with the usual way of doing things. Yellow curiosity was kept in check by the purple-blue desire to keep things ticking along as usual. Here and there, however, an aqua view of the big picture could be discerned—for instance in the acquisition of Gyrosta, which was supposed to introduce some of the missing capacity for innovation.

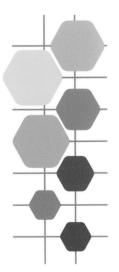

Gyrosta's cultural pattern

Gyrosta was founded as a start-up by three college students in Stockholm. In the few years of the company's existence, it had already won several awards for its innovative remote control systems, and had grown to a staff of 120.

Its rapid growth notwithstanding, Gyrosta was proud still to be functioning much like the start-up it had begun as. The company's culture was marked by a strong pattern of orange, yellow, and aqua memes. Like in its founding days, Gyrosta cultivated a dynamic, free-spirited atmosphere that kept breeding new ideas and visions. Thinking outside the box was the norm here. There were many informal workshops and ambitious brainstorming sessions in which no vision was too grand and no idea too bold.

Whereas aqua and yellow memes promoted intellectual rigor and long-term, future-oriented thinking, orange memes supported their practical implementation. Products and services could thus be launched onto the market quickly. That mistakes might happen in the process and customers' blue expectations of quality could not always be met was accepted as a consequence. Gyrosta was led by the three founding partners, each of whom headed a team as a functional unit. Channels of communication and decision-making were short and largely determined by the demands of the matter at hand. Little attention was paid to political considerations.

Mutual perception

The two future partners' cultural patterns analyzed above underscored what management already sensed: that the different ways of perceiving things might impede mutual understanding and breed conflict.

Maschinen-bau thinks it is ...		... but Gyrosta regards it as	Gyrosta thinks it is		... but Maschinenbau regards it as
structured	⬡	bureaucratic	smart	⬡	arrogant
disciplined	⬡⬡	dictatorial	ambitious	⬡	megaloma-niacal
grounded	⬡⬡	simple	visionary	⬡⬡⬡	dreaming
experienced	⬡⬡	old-fashioned	flexible	⬡⬡	chaotic
like a family	⬡	like a cult	thought-out	⬡⬡	theoretical

The process of integration

As a crucial challenge for the immediate future, the management of Maschinen-bau and Gyrosta identified not endangering the strengths of the recently acquired start-up by the merger. A full integration would mean that Gyrosta's young, dynamic culture was simply absorbed by the culture prevailing at Maschinenbau. If the latter's blue standards were simply imposed on Gyrosta, it would soon lose its orange-yellow capacity for innovation.

Prediction:	Gyrosta today	Gyrosta in five years' time	Gyrosta in ten years' time
Natural assimilation without coun-termeasures	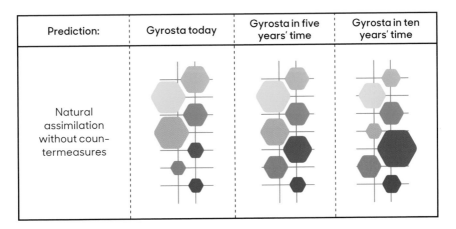		

A decision was thus made against full integration. Instead, the two companies were to work together in close partnership.

Culture Control

To bolster this partnership and simultaneously to preserve the strengths of both cultures, the management decided on the following measures:

- *Create cultural awareness:* Key players in both organizations analyzed and discussed existing cultural patterns. A broad awareness of the two different mindsets was cultivated. It became clear, what these differences meant for working and being successful together.
- *Take differences seriously:* Both companies recognized the opportunities offered by their cooperation and, particularly, that the greatest potential

for success lay in their difference. This was the foundation for tolerance and mutual respect.

- *Ensure respect for independence:* Even after the merger, Gyrosta's management was able to make decisions independently—albeit in close coordination with the new owners. Gyrosta's freedoms were not curtailed by standards already established at Maschinenbau. Instead, Gyrosta was able to adopt, of its own initiative, those standards of Maschinenbau that it considered fit and helpful in promoting growth.
- *Establish a code of conduct:* Both companies jointly developed a code of conduct, including guidelines for communication and coordination, which would determine cooperation in the subsequent years.

The cultural patterns of a university department

The situation: The department of organization and leadership at a medium-sized university was looking to take its ideas out of the ivory tower and into the marketplace.

The department consisted of two older professors and one younger, as well as two assistants. A few months ago, they all had embarked on the project with great enthusiasm, but it had gotten off to a rocky start. The task now was to find out whether the department's culture was already fit for this undertaking. With this in mind, its members used the Culture Map to reflect on the team's capabilities.

Analysis of the department's culture

In considering its culture, the team came to the realization that it was largely dominated by three colors: yellow, aqua, and green. The three dominant meme clusters were mutually reinforcing. Yellow thirst for knowledge was virtually limitless, the aqua field of vision kept expanding, and green memes ensured that any insights won were discussed exhaustively. One expression of this were workshops lasting entire weekends, during which any topic could be examined from the most diverse perspectives in a highly congenial atmosphere.

Business Culture Design

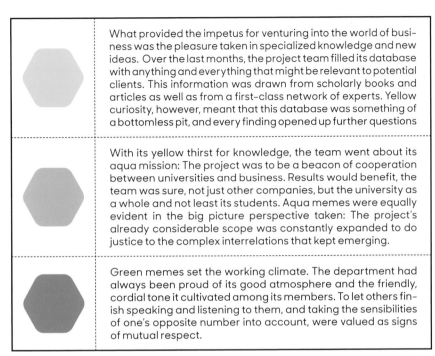

	What provided the impetus for venturing into the world of business was the pleasure taken in specialized knowledge and new ideas. Over the last months, the project team filled its database with anything and everything that might be relevant to potential clients. This information was drawn from scholarly books and articles as well as from a first-class network of experts. Yellow curiosity, however, meant that this database was something of a bottomless pit, and every finding opened up further questions
	With its yellow thirst for knowledge, the team went about its aqua mission: The project was to be a beacon of cooperation between universities and business. Results would benefit, the team was sure, not just other companies, but the university as a whole and not least its students. Aqua memes were equally evident in the big picture perspective taken: The project's already considerable scope was constantly expanded to do justice to the complex interrelations that kept emerging.
	Green memes set the working climate. The department had always been proud of its good atmosphere and the friendly, cordial tone it cultivated among its members. To let others finish speaking and listening to them, and taking the sensibilities of one's opposite number into account, were valued as signs of mutual respect.

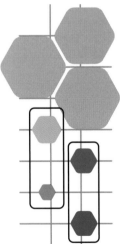

However, the Culture Map analysis soon made the team aware that it was lacking two crucial factors for ultimate success in the marketplace. Although its cultural pattern was able to generate creative ideas and theoretically sound concepts, there was a problem with putting them into practice. The lofty heights reached in workshop discussions were too remote from the labors of the plain. There were barely any orange or red memes to push for results: Orange pragmatism would have encouraged the prioritization of necessary activities; red determination would have put a stop to long-winded discussions. This would surely have spoiled the harmonious working atmosphere so treasured by all—but with good reason, as far as speed and results were concerned.

The underdevelopment of blue and purple memes was evident in the implementation of agreed measures. Instead of rigorously ticking off a job's components one by one, the entire package was constantly questioned. Everybody was reluctant to submit to the strictures of a concrete task.

Culture Control

Addressing its prevailing cultural pattern led the team to decide on a new working structure. Instead of working together on everything, tasks were divided into packages, to be the responsibility of individual team members. The holistic weekend workshops, though highly popular, were limited to twice a year. Instead, the focus was on short coordination meetings following a clear agenda and where binding goals were agreed on, according to professional principles. Timeframes were purposely kept narrow, in order to limit exhaustive green discussions and promote individual responsibility over lengthy coordination loops.

The team recognized that, though these measures were uncomfortable and did not meet their highest scholarly standards, they ultimately represented an important enhancement of the team's culture with a view to breaking into the world of business.

The former monopolist

The situation: Monopoprint was an institution among printers. The company's success was based on a utilization of capacities that remained constant and reliable for decades, but also depended on regular orders from state-run businesses. Phone books and railway timetables were particular reliable money-spinners. Digitalization and the mobile internet, however, reduced demand for printed products of that kind. The company had no choice but to reorient itself if it was going to keep its organism alive. As a part of developing a new strategy, the company used the Culture Map to understand its existing culture.

Cultural patterns

Established purple memes testify to the fact that Monopoprint's staff were accustomed to continuity. Any questions that arose were referred to the owner, whose decision was binding. Since he had always shown concern for his staff's wellbeing, his judgment enjoyed widespread acceptance. The workforce knew that management had their backs.

Green memes complemented the familial atmosphere at Monopoprint. The mood was good, staff were on friendly terms and enjoyed talking to one another. There was not a hint of dissension. Nobody could even remember when a worker had last been sacked.

While purple and green memes regulated the human aspects of working together, the company's business policies followed blue lines. Products and services offered were described as clearly as jobs and their responsibilities. Outside impulses, be it an order or an inquiry, set in motion well-defined processes that took care of the task step by step.

Together, the purple, blue, and green memes formed a mighty bulwark against change. A world without phone books and train schedules was simply impossible to imagine—as was a world without Monopoprint.

The left-hand side of the Culture Map, by contrast, was largely underdeveloped. Personal initiative or responsibility were not part of the company's repertoire. There were barely any yellow memes that might have kept an eye open for new technologies or questioned settled ways of doing things. Orange entrepreneurial spirit, too, was nipped in the bud by the dominant cultural pattern's overweening right-hand side. Only red memes displayed a little more force: especially, however, when it came to defending old privileges.

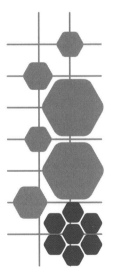

Closer scrutiny of the culture revealed another pattern: The purple memes acted with reference less to the company as a whole than to its various divisions. In other words, the kingdom of Monopoprint was divided into several duchies, each ruled by a powerful head of department. It was not least due to stable conditions and good sales that such silos could form. The well-developed green memes may have prevented the eruption of open conflict, but departmental boundaries came to mark the limits of one's own perception. What happened in other departments or if anyone needed support was largely unknown or simply of no interest.

Little surprise, then, that barely any aqua memes were to be found in this cultural pattern: Monopoprint lived in isolation from its environment. Orange impulses from the market side, like observing new trends and responding by developing new products, was as little in evidence as yellow pleasure in progress

With the results of the cultural analysis and the potentially lethal recent drop in sales in mind, the owner realized that a reorientation of the company could succeed only if it was accompanied by a break with cultural habits. His appeals for fundamental change were initially welcomed by all involved. But it soon emerged that they were merely lip service: the company's culture remained firmly in its comfort zone and all initiatives for change soon ran aground.

As a consequence, the owner reluctantly decided that only personnel changes could turn things around. A combination of internal changes and external additions was to bring about a cultural transformation. Carriers of orange memes within the company were sought, and two fairly young staff members entrusted with positions of responsibility, promotion to which would have taken rather longer if conventional paths had been adhered to. In addition, new staff were hired, some of whom had no experience in the printing business. They were to bring a breath of fresh air and new memes to the company. Parallel to the reassignment of tasks, the pay system was modified. The blue structure of jobs and processes with fixed salaries attached to every level was replaced by a performance-oriented approach with a high proportion of variable pay.

However, there was one thing for which the owner did not have the heart: To release his departmental "dukes" from their oaths of fealty—too strong was the feeling of mutual loyalty. He thus tried to redefine their tasks in a series of one-on-one meetings. Not in all cases did this succeed: Two heads of department resigned in disappointment.

This tough line came as a shock to many in the firm, the owner's many hints at the gravity of the situation notwithstanding. It took a while for people to get used to the new way of doing things at Monopoprint. Many staff missed the "good old days", and several quit. Yet overall, the number of employees remained constant. And as success returned to the company, new habits formed and with them, a new identity.

Selective Business Culture Design

Business Culture Design need not mean a fundamental and all-encompassing transformation of a company's culture. The approach can also help to identify a culture's patterns as they play out in relation to a particular subject or situation. The focus here is less on cultural developments that run deep in an organization than on the selective control of behavior—aware that behavior, as it becomes habitual within a collective, forms culture. With regard to specific challenges facing management and leadership, the question that arises is: Which memes ought to be activated in a particular situation? Individual hexagons of the Culture Map are thus used to encourage certain leadership behaviors in certain situations, much as landscape gardeners will often enhance the whole by placing particular accents in well-chosen spots.

In this way, Business Culture Design can help people in organizations to use particular hexagons to orient their behavior in given situations. In other words: Tools are chosen from a particular compartment. For instance, where feedback is concerned, strongly green organizations are better at empathy, strongly red ones at openness. But the need for both is something leaders can actively guide in terms of the hexagons. Similarly, a strongly orange-red culture can be reminded not to forget blue boundaries when setting itself targets.

Business Culture Design offers help in a broad range of typical situations in the practice of management and leadership. To illustrate, I have chosen a few examples:

A mission with a purpose

A company mission pointing to the organization's purpose has become one of the key control elements in businesses. It addresses both dimensions of business culture design: It enhances functionality and creates attractiveness—but only if it is actually in evidence in a company's culture, is part of lived experience.

The "organization's purpose" refers to the pattern that becomes visible when, at a distance, one looks at the individual goals pursued by people who have come together in an organization. No doubt these goals will never be completely identical, but they can be made to converge quite closely.

Problems arise when people within an organization pursue very different or even contradictory goals—if, for instance, some want to be a premium manufacturer offering the best possible product for the luxury end of the market, while others would prefer to reach the masses by means of lower prices.

Henry Ford saw it as the purpose of his company to build cars for ordinary people, not just a privileged few. That was the purpose, the "why" of the Ford Motor Company. Ikea, too, is guided by a purpose, "to create a better everyday life for the many people."[149] The idea is "to offer a wide range of well-designed, functional home furnishing products at prices so low that as many people as possible will be able to afford them." Ikea's everyday activities are to orient themselves by this idea. All decisions, be they in connection with investments, suppliers, manufacturing, or store design, must be measured accordingly. All the company's staff can consider their actions and decisions in its light. It would not occur to anybody at Ikea to offer an exclusive, luxury product, let alone in only a limited production run. That kind of thing is simply not the organization's purpose.

When I ask managers in seminars what a business's purpose is, I often hear replies like "making a profit" or "earning money." These are deeply orange answers. And of course, profits are a good thing—nothing wrong with that! Every business needs money to be able to invest in its future. When the money runs out, the organization starves, just like an organism starves for want of food. But does that make eating the purpose of life? Such an attitude would most likely not serve our organism's viability. For businesses, profits may be vital, but they are not the first cause. They are not the purpose, but the outcome.

Peter Drucker offers a widely recognized axiom: "There is only one valid definition of business purpose: to create a customer."[150] Ideally, one might add, several of them. No customers, no business—and certainly no profit. Sam Walton, the founder of Walmart, knew something similar when he kept reminding his organization of the customer's power: "He can fire everybody in the company from the chairman on down, simply by spending his money somewhere else."[151]

In the most general terms, for an organization to create a customer means having an idea for a product or a service, making it a reality, and selling somebody the result. In order to do so, however, the result must have a value. The purpose of a company is thus to create value for somebody outside the company. There is a markedly aqua component to such a definition.

Simon Sinek, a legend on the TED circuit, emphasizes that you can

Create value for others

hardly expect anyone to be thrilled by your product or service if you are not your-self convinced of your *why*, your reason for doing things.[152] Richard Branson, too, sees his Virgin Group's orange business ambitions as being tied to a higher purpose:

"At Virgin, we've always been driven by 'why'. [...] We've never gone into business solely to make money. We always start out to create something that is missing from the market, which will shake up the industry, and enable us and our customer to have fun in the process. We launched Virgin Records to give music lovers an easier and more enjoyable way to indulge in their passion, because we too loved music. We entered the airline industry with one plane and a dream to make air travel enter-taining, glamorous and to add a superior service—because we too desired change."[153]

Many business founders and start-ups have a clear idea of an aqua purpose in mind. In large corporations, keeping this higher purpose in mind is far more dif-ficult. What is more, it's not set in stone. It indicates the direction in which poten-tial customers may be found. The problem is that, where customers still crowded yesterday may today lie desolate. From time to time, then, a company's purpose and hence also its orientation must change. For a long time, Microsoft's mission was to put "a computer on every desk and in every home."[154] No doubt that was a good mission in the 1990s. Today, however, the tech industry finds itself compet-ing for dominance not over desks, but phones and even cars. In 2013, Microsoft's CEO Steve Ballmer finally announced the new mission: To "create a family of devices and services for individuals and businesses that empower people around the globe at home, at work and on the go, for the activities they value most."[155]

Yet even a good mission is not a guarantee for success, it can only point in the right direction. The culture as a whole decides what the results will be. Edwin Land, the inventor and founder of Polaroid, once proclaimed that his camera would "go beyond amusement and record-making to become a continuous partner of most human beings ... a new eye, and a second memory."[156] The company went bust, even though such a mission statement would not sound out of place in the smartphone era. Numerous apps serve exactly the purpose to which Polaroid once rallied.

There can be no doubt that a good mission contains a good shot of aqua: It creates meaning, creates value for others, orchestrates individual contributions and adapts to a changing environment. At the same time, it forms a reciprocal relationship with all the other colors:

	The mission is powerless as long as it exists only in an individual's brain. Only when the collective believes in the higher purpose can everybody rely on one another. At the same time, a common purpose creates a common identity. Differences recede into the background when people pursue a common mission.
	The path to the mission requires courage and resolve. The mission sets the direction and the red bulldozer has no time to waste: Decisions are soon followed by action—all the more important for the direction to be right.
	Blue planning and coordination can be helpful in pursuing the mission. Which structures, processes, and rules are helpful and which ones may once have been helpful but today are something of a hindrance is best considered from the perspective of the mission overall.
	Orange business-mindedness adds momentum in pursuit of the goal. The mission joins individual orange ambitions together, making individual goals converge on a single, overarching objective.
	The mission needs to convince people not just on a rational level, but on an emotional one, too. An idealistic mission also activates green memes, which then wholeheartedly support the higher purpose.
	The yellow spirit of discovery finds the new solutions that a visionary purpose needs. Yellow thirst for knowledge goes deep. The mission helps it decide where to go deep and directs attention toward competent partners with whom to exchange knowledge.

Business Culture Design

Innovating patterns

An ample supply of orange memes in a culture ensures that an organization keeps on wanting to improve. They are an important driver for successful innovating. With regard to the question how companies push forward the subject of innovation, two typical patterns can be distinguished: incremental innovation and radical innovation.

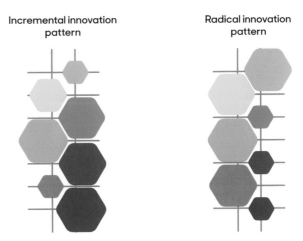

The goal of incremental innovation is to offer the customer an optimized product or service in the future: The new sports car will offer faster acceleration with lower fuel consumption, the new home internet contract provides faster transmission of more data at a lower cost, the new milk carton comes with an improved screw-top, and bedding is made cheaper by an improved supply and delivery chain. An existing solution, in other words, is refined, while the core that defines the product or service remains unaltered. Offerings are gradually improved, but the market, customers, and competitors remain largely the same.

Radical innovation, on the other hand, departs from existing technologies. Whereas incremental innovations can build on the company's experience to success, radical innovation breaks completely new ground. The cards are completely reshuffled. Radical innovations are life-changing not just for customers, but also for the competition. Automobiles meant that horse-drawn carriages were no longer a commonplace sight in cities, computers hastened the obsolescence of typewriters, and digital cameras replaced analog photography.

Through the lens of the Culture Map, we can identify different patterns that typically underlie incremental and radical innovation. Both possess a strong entrepreneurial orange. That aside, however, clear differences are evident.

 Orange memes are strongly developed in both patterns, thus providing an important precondition for successful innovation. They testify to a desire for improvement, the urge to win. With an eye on the market, changes are observed, opportunities recognized, and solutions developed.

Additionally, experience, reliable processes, and participation have an important part to play in the pattern of incrementally innovating culture:

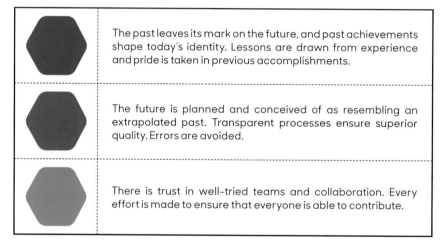

The past leaves its mark on the future, and past achievements shape today's identity. Lessons are drawn from experience and pride is taken in previous accomplishments.

The future is planned and conceived of as resembling an extrapolated past. Transparent processes ensure superior quality. Errors are avoided.

There is trust in well-tried teams and collaboration. Every effort is made to ensure that everyone is able to contribute.

Alongside orange, these three hexagons allow a continuous improvement of existing services and products. However, it is rare for radically new things to emerge from such a pattern.

The pattern of radical innovation typically reveals three quite different hexagons and their associated memes behind the strong orange. Driven by a strong mission, they know neither fear, nor taboo, nor compromise in their attempt to change the world.

Whereas the right-hand, communally minded side of the Culture Map supports the orange ambitions of incrementally innovating cultures, it is the left-

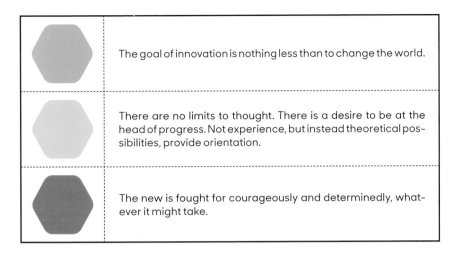

	The goal of innovation is nothing less than to change the world.
	There are no limits to thought. There is a desire to be at the head of progress. Not experience, but instead theoretical possibilities, provide orientation.
	The new is fought for courageously and determinedly, whatever it might take.

hand, individualistic side that calls the tune in radically innovating companies. Here, it is above all the aqua vision that holds together cultures that otherwise consist largely of lone wolves. What is more, yellow-aqua dreams are supported by red courage and determination, which help them become true. In the radical pattern, a strongly red drive cancels out risk perception. The culture takes pleasure in casting off old ways and breaking new ground.

Behind the incrementally innovating pattern, on the other hand, you will find great reserves of expertise and know-how with regard to products, services, and customers. There is strong reliance on established processes and trusted people. This cultural pattern, containing a lot of purple, blue, and green, often contains an important trove of experience. Such a treasure can, however, turn out to be a burden when it comes to creating something really fundamentally new.

Phases of deep change often spell chances for newcomers to take the lead. Experienced incumbents do not always succeed at reorienting themselves and defending their market-leading position. Newcomers face the challenge of ensuring qualitative reliability by constantly optimizing their offerings with orange and blue memes, whereas established players need to increase their yellow and aqua activities if they are not to fall by the wayside before the next quantum leap. The automobile industry provides an instructive example for these differing approaches to innovation, which can be identified in the fields of alternative drive systems and new mobility concepts.

While the established manufacturers were still adding to their lists of thousands of reasons why electric cars would never work, let alone with a mass market, a complete nobody called Tesla set about disproving them. For Tesla's memes were different, largely yellow and aqua, with a good dose of red boldness and entrepreneurial orange. Founder Elon Musk's aqua vision was to improve the world by making electric cars affordable to all. In addition, he took his sober yellow bearings by science and logic. At the established carmakers, Musk's plans for the future were met by purple experience, nearly perfect blue processes, and well-functioning green teams. Their corporate cultures were dominated by long histories of success. Perception was filtered through a belief in horsepower and torque. It took some years for them to wake up and take their new competitor seriously.

For radical innovation, it is advisable rigorously to separate the old from the new. A new line of business will often require new strategies and goals, new organizational structures, and new leadership. Not infrequently, new staff will also be needed here and there. In any case, this organism requires a new way of thinking, a new culture.

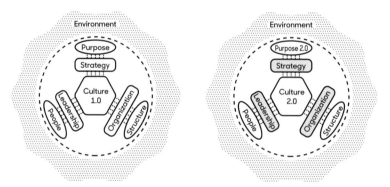

This split allows for the formation of a new organism, left to develop its own culture unburdened and unrestricted. Once the new organism has established itself, it can be reintegrated into the original one—or can become a new business and as such another pillar of the company, exist in parallel, or even come to replace the old business model.

Many companies have such thoughts in mind when they set innovative projects free from traditional structures. For instance, BMW's start-up Garage allows young and innovative companies to cooperate with the legacy carmaker while retaining their own culture.[157]

Business Culture Design

Management by Objectives and Self-Control

One of the most popular and successful management concepts is Management by Objectives and Self-Control (MbO). The ideas underpinning it go back to Peter Drucker, who argued that a company's objective needed to be broken down for individual managers.[158]

Everybody in an organization has something different to contribute to the common goal. Yet each performance must point in the same direction so that individual contributions produce a greater whole.

In practice, unfortunately, all we see often is the first half, i.e. management by setting objectives; the self-control part is all too often ignored. Not infrequently, the MbO process is dominated by blue memes. Not only are objectives set in a top-down manner, but also the way to get there. The construct remains rigid in spite of the context having changed. For Peter Drucker, however, objectives and self-control went hand in hand: People were not only to have tar-

	Agreed-on objectives show people in an organization what is expected of them and what they are measured by, allowing them to control their own performance and set their own priorities.
	Individual actions become contributions to the whole if they serve the organization's purpose. An aqua view of the entire organization is also necessary in order to orient and combine individual contributions, and consequently to define the appropriate individual goals.
	Since orange pragmatism can sometimes be too flexible on its way to the goal, it is important to set clear ground rules for all involved to adhere to. Blue boundaries demonstrate what is and what is not permissible. Within these limits, the path to the objective may be chosen freely.
	Objectives should ideally be set based on green consensus. Managers should be involved in developing objectives, for individuals should not only know their goals, but also be convinced by them.

gets to give them a sense of direction, but were also to be given the possibility to attain them by their own initiative.

Well-functioning Management by Objectives and Self-Control naturally reveals many orange memes, though an aqua orientation and blue rules are also part of it, as is a dose of green on the path to agreeing on objectives.

A well-designed MbO process allows individuals to demonstrate initiative and contribute autonomously to an overarching objective. As the best-selling author Daniel Pink has argued in *Drive*, this is especially motivating. He identifies autonomy, mastery, and purpose as crucial motives for performance—more effective, in many cases, than monetary incentives.[159] Self-determination, and finding the way to the goal by one's own lights, is an important orange meme—as is the pleasure in constantly getting better at something. Aqua meaningfulness sets the course: to improve products, services, and even the world. These three aspects foster ambition, commitment, and not least a willingness to change.

The popular concept of Objectives and Key Results (OKR) follows a logic quite similar to MBO at first sight, but with some crucial differences:[160] The orange key results provide measurable outcomes on the way to the objectives, which are ambitiously not set top-down but largely emerge bottom-up. A red dose of boldness is encouraged. In addition, OKRs emphasize the yellow aspect of learning, incorporated by transparency and frequent collaborative exchange.

Multi-dimensional trust

"Trust is good, control is better" is a quote often attributed to Lenin. And for sure, it's better to be safe than sorry. Countless managers have made the experience that trust is all very well and good, but it is better to check and verify that instructions are being fulfilled. For a long time, it was indeed possible to run an organization more or less in line with this principle. The fact that this is ever less the case is certainly not due to a lack of means of verification. In fact, thanks to technological progress, there are more of them than ever.

Improved means of monitoring notwithstanding, trust remains a crucial factor, not least on account of growing complexity in and around organizations. It becomes particularly important when things get incomprehensible or unpredictable. If it is difficult to understand behavior, trust is needed. And let's be honest: Nobody likes being monitored all the time anyway.

It is not without reason that business leaders, staff, and countless management experts recommend establishing a culture of trust. But what are the core elements of such a culture?

	Trust is often discussed in relation to only one dimension: trust in a human relationship. This trust holds that all involved will behave with integrity and loyalty, in good faith and to the best of their knowledge. Everyone can be sure of being neither deceived nor cheated by anyone else, not least out of decency and mutual respect. This dimension of trust is founded on green memes.
	In a business context, a second dimension is just as important to a stable culture of trust: trust in performance and results. Trust is placed in the commitment of others to work towards the agreed objectives. Trust becomes confidence.
	Finally, there is a blue dimension to a healthy culture of trust: trust in agreements. Blue memes ensure that people stick to agreements. Reliability thus produces trust.

If only one of these dimensions is weak, there is little for a culture of trust to stand on. If there is no relying on performance, no real trust will ever emerge. What is more, it is hard to trust somebody with a good work ethic and personal integrity, yet who keeps breaking agreements. Finally, trust cannot emerge where there is reason to doubt personal relationships. To expect a knife in one's back at the first opportunity points to severe issues of trust. Depending on which dimension is lacking, it may be specifically addressed with the aim of creating a stable culture of trust.

Caring and candid feedback

In dealing with one another, people often confront a dilemma: a good atmosphere or open conflict? When designing their feedback culture, companies often end up too close to one extreme on a scale running from red to green.

Yet good feedback is priceless, as I myself discovered: As a young consultant, many of the business's ways and customs were new to me. I worked and tried hard —but not everything went as I hoped. One day, a colleague took me aside. He told me that my concept papers did not conform to expectations in terms of structure and layout. I resolved to be more careful in future. Another few weeks later, however, my colleague was frank with me: Structure and layout of my concepts were simply abominable! His feedback was so clear that it took me a few days to get over my wounded pride. But after a few days off sulking, I took his criticism to heart and reworked my concepts from the bottom up. I made a close study of the guidelines, asked colleagues for advice, rolled up my sleeves and was able to improve my results significantly. Looking back, I was very grateful to my colleague for his caring green interest in my development, but also for his red directness.

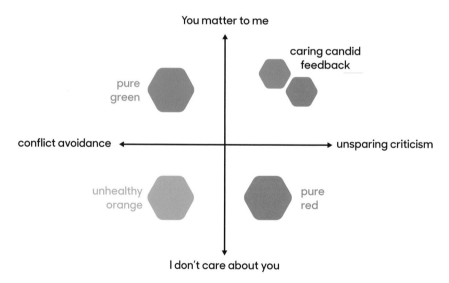

Business Culture Design

Broadly speaking, feedback cultures can be classified along two axes:[161] The Y-axis plots whether somebody personally cares about somebody else or not. The X-axis runs from conflict avoidance to unsparing criticism, of the kind that doesn't mind annoying or even hurting another.

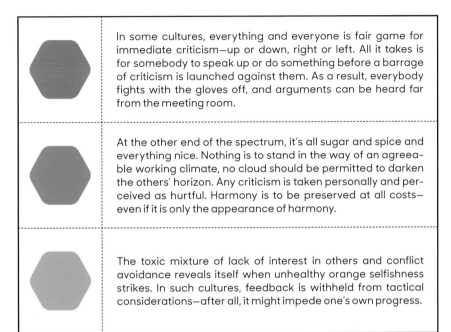

	In some cultures, everything and everyone is fair game for immediate criticism—up or down, right or left. All it takes is for somebody to speak up or do something before a barrage of criticism is launched against them. As a result, everybody fights with the gloves off, and arguments can be heard far from the meeting room.
	At the other end of the spectrum, it's all sugar and spice and everything nice. Nothing is to stand in the way of an agreeable working climate, no cloud should be permitted to darken the others' horizon. Any criticism is taken personally and perceived as hurtful. Harmony is to be preserved at all costs—even if it is only the appearance of harmony.
	The toxic mixture of lack of interest in others and conflict avoidance reveals itself when unhealthy orange selfishness strikes. In such cultures, feedback is withheld from tactical considerations—after all, it might impede one's own progress.

Good feedback cultures achieve the balance between green and red. They manage to be both humane and though. People don't just have their own careers in mind. They care about others, too—to the point of rubbing them the wrong way. Even without being asked, they give each other feedback in a spirit of caring candor. If green memes are in short supply, an aggressive culture will develop, in which everybody is quick to criticize anybody, meanly and cruelly. In the absence of red memes, everything turns to cotton candy, and superficial harmony forbids any criticism. Depending on what is lacking, leaders can make corrections in one direction or another.

Culture-conscious meeting management

Companies invest a considerable part of their resources in meetings—their staff's time, that is. Senior managers sometimes spend two thirds of their working time in meetings, middle managers around half.[162] This means that spending 25 to 30 hours a week in meetings is far from rare. If four people get together for one hour, that means half of one person's working day is invested. If you add preparation time and time after the meeting for minutes etc., you will soon reach a full working day. At the same time, participants often complain about rather underwhelming results or entirely superfluous meetings. Yet it is not only the financial cost of meetings that should be borne in mind. Psychologists have concluded that too many badly planned meetings are not just a nuisance, but unhealthy into the bargain. Meetings really *can make you sick*![163]

It is not up to chance whether or not an organization falls into unhealthy meeting habits. Here, too, habits become established over time, and the hexagons of the Culture Map can help mold them deliberately. Every meeting is governed by the most diverse of memes—but are they really the most helpful ones in that situation?

Yellow creativity is essential to brainstorming meetings. But if it's just about giving short status updates, the rigid timing of blue is in order. Orange should not be left out when practical solutions are being sought. In meetings, too, context decides what the appropriate mix of colors is.

Meetings usually begin outside the conference room, with the invitation and the distribution of the agenda. What are the expected results and what skills are needed? Orange and yellow considerations can help answer this question: Orange memes have the goal firmly in sight and set priorities, while yellow memes soberly take stock of skills and knowledge rather than personal preferences in choosing participants for a particular meeting. Ideally, all participants should be informed of the meeting's purpose well in advance—a modicum of aqua should not be asking too much.

Furthermore, an organization's well-worn cultural pattern also influences what is to be borne in mind when calling a meeting and who is to be invited. In purple cultures, besides the chieftains, such influence can also be in the hands of informal potentates. To exclude them is to endanger the implementation of the meeting's outcomes. In strongly blue cultures, it is important to invite everybody who is formally supposed to be invited. Anyone looking to keep the number of participants down in the name of efficiency and to streamline proceedings will have their work cut out in a green culture, where suddenly being highly selective will ruffle many feathers.

In the meeting itself, blue principles have an important part to play. Between its punctual beginning and end, a meeting needs rules and structures to which all adhere: from the agenda via the priority accorded individual points to the minutes, where binding decisions ought to be recorded. The clearer the structures, the less need there is for a purple-red chair to rule over the meeting with a firm hand.

Depending on the matters at hand, it may be worth paying special attention to the balance between yellow and aqua, that is to say, decide whether the focus is to be on details or the greater whole. There can indeed be meetings in which specialists can fine-tune the details of a matter. All the more important, then, to ensure that all contributions can subsequently fit in an overall aqua context.

As with giving feedback, it is important to find the right balance between red and green during the meeting, for neither red argumentativeness nor superficial green consensus really help reach the best solution. A viable consensus can be reached only where constructive dissent is voiced. Alfred P. Sloan, Jr., the former head of General Motors, knew how important dissenting voices are. He is reported to have admonished his colleagues in a meeting of senior managers:[164] "Gentlemen, I take it we are all in complete agreement on the decision here." Everybody nodded in agreement. Sloan continued: "Then I propose we postpone further discussion of this matter until our next meeting to give ourselves time to develop disagreement and perhaps gain some understanding of what the decision is all about."

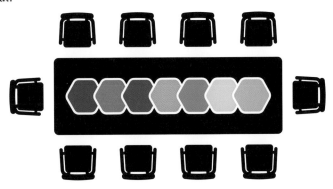

Depending on how the meeting goes, it may be necessary consciously to foreground a particular hexagon and its memes. I know organizations in which it is customary to put differently colored hexagons on the table in order to help participants find the perspective appropriate to the phase the meeting is in.

It is legitimate to interrupt interminable yellow-green discussions with a red intervention, at least from time to time. If the actual matter in hand is in danger of falling by the wayside, you would do well to remind everybody of the orange objective or the aqua purpose. Some meetings are about yellow facts, others about the blue process. But green community and purple belonging are also vital components of a good meeting culture. All hexagons can be useful. The point is to apply them in the right place and at the right time.

The iceberg I mentioned in Chapter 1 can also be found in meetings: There is visible behavior, and there are unseen motivations. Not always is it possible to make immediate sense of the symptoms that reveal themselves in meetings. If, for instance, a superficial but flimsy consensus becomes apparent in the unopposed acceptance of decisions, the causes may be manifold and not instantly recognizable: Green memes may be suppressing dissent in order to safeguard harmony. Purple memes trust the patriarch implicitly—and if they are joined by orange memes, the whole table will soon be nodding its opportunistic assent. Blue memes are unlikely to question decisions from above as a matter of principle. Aqua memes may simply fail to recognize the relevance of a decision and instead turn to seemingly more pressing matters.

No question: you can use the hexagons to control behavior and thereby improve your meeting culture. Beyond that, however, it helps to identify and understand the powerful underlying cultural patterns. For this is how the fundamental drivers can be used and consciously developed.

Business Culture Design

Acknowledgements

In a sense, the book you are holding in your hands resembles the iceberg from chapter 1: here, too, there is much that remains unseen. Many invisible factors make up a book and contribute to its inception, planning, writing, and design. I would like to take this opportunity to thank the many people without whom *Business Culture Design* could probably never have been completed in its present form.

The Culture Map was brought to life by working in and alongside many organizations. I would like to thank them all for their trust, for the valuable insights they gave me into so many different corporate cultures, and for the opportunity to work collaboratively on such a variety of exciting topics.

My partners at The Culture Institute in Zurich help our clients develop their corporate cultures. They bring passion and commitment to every one of them—and to the application and continuing development of Business Culture Design. I would particularly like to thank Frank Hermle for his valuable contributions to this book and for an amazing working partnership.

Rita J. King and James Jorasch of Science House in New York continue to enrich the idea of the Culture Map with their imaginative innovations, practical experience, and not least their inspiring thoughts. What began as a transatlantic, project-based R&D partnership has grown into a valuable friendship. Thank you so much!

Reza Razavi is an inspiring thinker about culture and the future, and I would like to thank him for his support as a sparring partner, his bold ideas, and the innovative approach he has brought to our joint work. Thanks are due also to Peter Eltze for our valuable conversations and for the inspiration he has brought to our culture projects.

My dissertation's academic and entrepreneurial fathers, Professor Stephan Laske and Urs Bolter, enabled me to bring science and its application together fruitfully in the Culture Map's original development. I would like to express my deep gratitude for their confidence, knowledge, and commitment.

From our first meeting, Michael Schickerling was convinced by my idea for this book, and I wish to thank him for supporting me in developing the concept and publication strategy. Desirée Šimeg brilliantly supported me in refining the book's outline and helping make it a reality, and finally for her hands-on support in editing the text. For the English translation, my thanks go to Joe Kroll for his competence, creativity, and perseverance.

In addition, I would like to thank my publishing team at Campus Verlag for their help and unwavering support, especially my editor, Stephanie Walter. Credit is due to the designers, Justin Colt and Jose Fresneda of The Collected Works, New York, for their illustrations and support in designing the cover. Thank you for your beautiful work!

I am particularly grateful to my family. My parents always encouraged me to explore the world, gather experiences, and cultivate new interests. Thank you for a lifetime's support of my activities!

Finally, this project could not have come to fruition without the loving support of my wife, Karolina. Whether I was abroad for a longer stretch of time or spent evenings and weekends working on the manuscript, I always felt safe in the knowledge that she shared my enthusiasm for this book.

Business Culture Design

Notes

1 Similar iceberg models appear in psychology as well as in theories of education and communication. With regard to corporate culture, the iceberg was popularized chiefly by Edgar Schein.

2 This quotation is often falsely ascribed to Peter Drucker. Its precise origin is unknown, and the Drucker Institute is equally unaware of its provenance.

3 Geert Hofstede, *Culture's Consequences*, second edition, 2001.

4 *Forbes*, "Steel versus Silicon," July 7, 1997, http://www.forbes.com/forbes/1997/0707/6001129a.html.

5 Heidi and Paul Senger-Weiss (eds.), *Das WeissBuch*, 2010.

6 Cyrus Achouri, *Wenn Sie wollen, nennen Sie es Führung*, 2011.

7 *Aviationfigure*, June 30, 2015, http://www.aviationgure.com/15-interesting-facts-about-airbus-a380/

8 Kerry A. Dolan, "The Soda With Buzz," *Forbes*, March 28, 2005, http://www.forbes.com/forbes/2005/0328/126.html

9 Bernhard Prangl, "Ein Phänomen unserer Zeit: Komplexität," http://www.dreipfeilerweg.com/ein-phaenomen-unserer-zeit-komplexitaet/#more-7059

10 Peter F. Drucker, "Will the corporation survive?", *The Economist*, November 1, 2001.

11 Peter M. Senge, *The Fifth Discipline: The Art and Practice of the Learning Organization*, 1990, p. 4.

12 Eric Schmidt and Jonathan Rosenberg, "How Google Works," October 12, 2014, https://www.slideshare.net/ericschmidt/how-google-works-final-1#12

13 Daniel Pink, *Drive*, 2009.

14 Rob Walker, "The Guts of a New Machine", The New York Times, November 30, 2003

15 Edgar H. Schein, *Organizational Culture and Leadership*, 4th edition, 2010.

16 Lou Gerstner Jr., *Who Says Elephants Can't Dance?*, 2002, p. 182.

17 Jared Diamond, *The Third Chimpanzee*, 1993.

18 Richard Dawkins, *The Selfish Gene*, Anniversary Edition, 2006, p. 245.

19 Steve Jobs (1995), *The Lost Interview*, documentary, 2012, https://www.youtube.com/watch?v=TRZAJY23xio,1h 04 min.

20 I base this distinction on the work of Jonnie Hughes, who uses these categories in his entertaining account of how a jellyfish, a sea slug, a chicken, and a human would cross a road. Jonnie Hughes, *On the Origin of Tepees*, 2011.

21 Richard Dawkins, *The Selfish Gene*, Anniversary Edition, 2006, ch. 11.

22 Richard Brodie, *Virus of the Mind*, 2009, p. 7.

23 Science has come to the conclusion that, in the course of evolution, human beings have also adopted genetic material from bacteria, probably transmitted by viruses. By far the larger part of genetic material is transmitted vertically, from one generation to the next, as it were top-down.

24 Fredmund Malik, *Management, das A und O des Handwerks*, 2007, p. 264

25 Lou Gerstner Jr., *Who Says Elephants Can't Dance?*, 2002, p. 117.

26 Daniel C. Dennett, *Darwin's Dangerous Idea*, 1995, p. 365.

27 Daniel C. Dennett, "The Evolution of Culture," in John Brockman (ed.), *Culture*, 2011.

28 A fitting term has emerged for the more or less humorous pictures circulating on the web: memes!

29 Frederic Vester, *Die Kunst vernetzt zu denken*, 2002, p. 22; Christian Becker-Carus: *Grundriß der physiologischen Psychologie*, 1981, p. 129.

30 Cyrus Achouri, *Wenn Sie wollen, nennen Sie es Führung*, p. 85.

31 Ray Mock, *Banksy in New York*, 2014.

32 Arte Sciences, *Wahrheit? Alles Lüge. Wie das Gehirn Wirklichkeit konstruiert*, 2007, https://www.youtube.com/watch?v=M1iDwL59CqA

33 Peter L. Berger, Thomas Luckmann, *The Social Construction of Reality*, 1966.

34 Cade Metz, "Tech Time Warp of the Week: Watch Steve Ballmer Laugh at the Original iPhone," *Wired*, May 9, 2014, http://www.wired.com/2014/09/tech-time-warp-of-the-week-watch-steve-ballmer-laugh-at-the-original-iphone/

35 Albert H. Hastorf, Hadley Cantril, "They saw a game," in *The Journal of Abnor-*

mal Psychology, 1954, http://www.all-about-psychology.com/support-les/selective-perception-they-saw-a-game.pdf

36 Clare W. Graves, "Human nature prepares for a momentous leap," in *The Futurist*, April 1974.

37 Christopher C. Cowan, Natasha Todorovic, *The Never Ending Quest: Dr. Clare W. Graves Explores Human Nature*, 2005.

38 Don Becks, Chris Cowan, *Spiral Dynamics*, 1996.

39 Ken Wilber, *A Theory of Everything*, 2001.

40 Said Elias Dawlabani, *MEMEnomics*, 2013.

41 Marion Küstenmacher, Tilmann Haberer, Werner Küstenmacher, *Gott 9.0*, 2010.

42 Christopher C. Cowan, Natasha Todorovic, *The Never Ending Quest: Dr. Clare W. Graves Explores Human Nature* p. vi,

43 Leading anthropologists, notably Franz Boas (1858–1942) and Margaret Mead (1901–1978), strictly opposed the idea that cultures developed in a particular direction.

44 Robert Wright, *Nonzero: The Logic of Human Destiny*, 1999, p. 17.

45 Geert Hofstede, *Culture's Consequences*, second edition, 2001, p. 209ff.

46 Jerker Denrell, "Selection Bias and the Perils of Benchmarking," in *Harvard Business Review* 83 (4), 2005.

47 Brian Chesky, "Don't Fuck Up the Culture," April 20, 2014, https://medium.com/@bchesky/dont-fuck-up-the-culture-597cde9ee9d4

48 Tony Hsieh, "Startup Growing Pains," *Stanford Technology Ventures Program*, 11. October 11, 2010, https://www.youtube.com/watch?v=F8k_tb13tAk

49 Tony Hsieh, "Your Culture Is Your Brand," *Huffington Post*, November 15, 2010, https://www.huffingtonpost.com/tony-hsieh/zappos-founder-tony-hsieh_1_b_783333.html

50 Hermann Simon, *Die heimlichen Gewinner*, 1996, p. 187.

51 Alexander Demling, "Zum Tod von Hans Riegel: Der Mann mit dem Bärenhunger," *Spiegel Online*, March 15, 2013, http://www.spiegel.de/wirtschaft/unternehmen/haribo-zum-tod-von-hans-riegel-a-927976.html

52 http://www.blum-ic.com/ueber-uns/wir-und-blum; "Ein Metaller für die Küche," *Der Standard*, April 3, 2015, http://derstandard.at/2000013737586/Vorarlberger-Traditionsbetrieb-Blum-Ein-Metaller-fuer-die-Kueche

53 BBC Two, "Make me a German," 21. August 2013, https://www.youtube.com/watch?v=mSQKtxJ-Uvk

54 Hermann Simon, *Hidden Champions: Aufbruch nach Globalia*, 2012

55 Jonathan Haidt, "How common threats can make common (political) ground," *TED Salon*, New York, 2012, https://www.ted.com/talks/jonathan_haidt_how_common_threats_can_make_common_political_ground/transcript?language=en

56 Joseph Schumpeter, *Capitalism, Socialism, and Democracy*, 1942.

57 Peter F. Drucker (1999), "Managing Oneself," in *Harvard Business Review*, January 2005.

58 Sergio Marchionne, "Fiat's Extreme Makeover," in: *Harvard Business Review*, December 2008, https://hbr.org/2008/12/Fiats-extreme-makeover

59 Jeffrey A. Krames, *The Jack Welch Lexicon of Leadership*, 2002, p. 35.

60 Ibid., p. 25.

61 Ibid., p. 8.

62 Martin Lindstrom, "The Truth About Being 'Done' Versus Being 'Perfect,'" in *Fast Company*, September 25, 2012, http://www.fastcompany.com/3001533/truth-about-being-done-versus-being-perfect

63 Reed Hastings, "Netflix Culture: Freedom & Responsibility," https://de.slideshare.net/reed2001/culture-2009/16-16CourageYou_say_what_you_think

64 Walter Isaacson, *Steve Jobs*, 2012, Ch. 1.1 ("The Reality Distortion Field").

65 Ibid., p. 118.

66 Jordan Belfort, Facebook, August 27, 2013, https://www.facebook.com/jordanbelfort/posts/10151941759793465

67 Jordan Belfort, Facebook, January 13, 2010, https://www.facebook.com/jordanbelfort/posts/275537340699

68 Walter Isaacson, *Steve Jobs*, p. 512.

69 "Big Brothers," in *Manager Magazin*, 7/2014, pp. 26–34.

70 http://www.haier.net/en/about_haier/news/201404/t20140426_218091.shtml

71 Niccolò Machiavelli, *The Prince*, 1532, http://www.bartleby.com/36/1/17.html

72 *House of Cards*, Ch. 14, season 2, ep. 1.

73 Arthur Schopenhauer, *On The Suffering of the World* (1819) 2004, p. 17.

74 Matthew Hutson, "Espousing Equality, but Embracing a Hierarchy," in *The New York Times*, June 21, 2014, http://www.nytimes.com/2014/06/22/business/espousing-equality-but-embracing-a-hierarchy.html

75 *"Wirtschaft und Gesellschaft – Max Weber,"* in *Handelsblatt Management Bibliothek – Teil L–Z: Die besten Managementbücher,* 2005, p. 243.

76 Duff McDonald, "The Making of McKinsey," 2013, https://blog.longreads.com/2013/10/23/the-making-of-mckinsey-a-brief-history-of-management/

77 *"Meine Jahre bei General Motors – Alfred Sloan,"* in *Handelsblatt Management Bibliothek – Teil L–Z: Die besten Managementbücher,* 2005, pp. 51ff.

78 *Handelsblatt Management Bibliothek,* vol. 5, 2005, *Die erfolgreichsten Unternehmer.*

79 Charlie Chaplin, *Modern Times,* 1936, https://www.youtube.com/watch?v=DfGs2Y5WJ14

80 "Was Wirtschaft treibt," in *brand eins,* 4/2014, p. 33.

81 Helmut Schmidt, *Lebensfragen,* 2013, documentary film.

82 Taiichi Ohno, *Toyota Production System: Beyond large-scale production,* 1993.

83 Adam Smith, *An Inquiry into the Nature and Causes of the Wealth of Nations,* 1776.

84 *Wall Street,* 1987 (dir. Oliver Stone).

85 Brad Smith, "Intuit's CEO on Building a Design-Driven Company," in *Harvard Business Review,* January 1, 2015, https://hbr.org/2015/01/intuits-ceo-on-building-a-design-driven-company

86 Brad Power and Steve Stanton, "How IBM, Intuit, and Rich Products Became More Customer-Centric," in *Harvard Business Review,* June 17, 2015, https://hbr.org/2015/06/how-ibm-intuit-and-rich-products-became-more-customer-centric

87 Bernd Venohr, *Wachsen wie Würth,* 2006.

88 Richard Branson, "Opportunity missed," 2012, https://www.virgin.com/richard-branson/opportunity-missed

89 Richard Branson, "My top 10 quotes on opportunity," 2015, https://www.virgin.com/richard-branson/my-top-10-quotes-on-opportunity

90 https://www.amazon.jobs/principles

91 Rita J. King, "Culture Controversy at Amazon, Decoded," August 17, 2015, https://www.linkedin.com/pulse/culture-controversy-amazon-decoded-rita-j-king.

92 Samuel Gibbs, "Jeff Bezos: I've made billions of dollars of failures at Amazon," in *The Guardian,* December 3, 2014, https://www.theguardian.com/technology/2014/dec/03/jeff-bezos-billions-dollars-failures-amazon

93 *Master of the Universe*, 2013 (dr. Marc Bauder).

94 https://en.wikiquote.org/wiki/Thomas_Edison

95 http://www.brainyquote.com/quotes/quotes/t/thomasaed149038.html

96 Martin Putschögl, Franziska Zoidl, "Airbnb: Vermieten in der Grauzone," in *DerStandard.at*, March 28, 2015, http://derstandard.at/2000013565755/Airbnb-Vermieten-in-der-Grauzone.

97 Greg Smith, "Why I am leaving Goldman Sachs," in *The New York Times*, March 14, 2012.

98 http://www.brainyquote.com/quotes/quotes/r/raykroc153490.html

99 Paul Lawrence, Nitin Nohria, *Driven, Was Menschen und Organisationen antreibt*, 2002, p. 89.

100 Max Frisch, *Siamo italiani—Die Italiener*, 1965.

101 http://www.starbucks.com/responsibility/community/diversity-and-inclusion/culture

102 http://www.starbucks.de/about-us/company-information/diversity-at-starbucks

103 https://www.southwest.com/html/about-southwest/careers/culture.html

104 Sigal Barsade, Olivia A. O'Neill, "Motor für die Leistung," in *Harvard Business Manager*, March 2016.

105 Daniel Goleman, "What makes a great leader?," in *Harvard Business Review*, November/December 1998.

106 Nicholas Carlson, "The Untold Story Of Larry Page's Incredible Comeback," in *Business Insider*, April 24, 2014, http://www.businessinsider.com/larry-page-the-untold-story-2014-4.

107 Charles Duhigg, "What google learned from its quest to build the perfect team," in *The New York Times Magazine*, February 25, 2016, http://www.nytimes.com/2016/02/28/magazine/what-google-learned-from-its-quest-to-build-the-perfect-team.html?_r=3

108 http://www.brunellocucinelli.com/en/philosophy#/page/7

109 Sabine Holzknecht, "Der gute Kapitalist," in *brand eins*, June 2014, http://www.brandeins.de/archiv/2014/geld/der-gute-kapitalist/

110 Matthias zur Bonsen, *Leading with life: Lebendigkeit im Unternehmen freisetzen und nutzen*, 2010, p. 228.

111 Matthias Kaufmann, "Der Waldorf-Discounter," in *Manager Magazin*,

February 5, 2004, http://www.manager-magazin.de/unternehmen/karri-ere/a-284159.html

112 Gabriele Fischer, "Die wichtigsten Kunden sind die Mitarbeiter – Interview mit Götz W. Werner," in *brand eins*, May 2014, http://www.brandeins.de/archiv/2014/im-interesse- des-kunden/die-wichtigsten-kunden-sind-die-mi-tarbeiter/

113 http://www.karl-valentin.de/zitate/zitate.htm

114 Saj-nicole Joni, DamonBeyer, "How to Pick a Good Fight," in *Harvard Business Review*, ecember 2009, https://hbr.org/2009/12/how-to-pick-a-good-fight

115 https://www.tofflerassociates.com/vanishing-point/organizational-learn-ing-is-the-key-to-solving-21st-century-issues

116 Georg Etscheit, "Der Tüftler im Glashaus," in *Die Zeit*, April 1, 2004, http://www.zeit.de/2004/15/M-Daimler

117 Nicholas Carlson, "The Untold Story of Larry Page's Incredible Comeback," in *Business Insider*, April 24, 2014, http://www.businessinsider.com/larry-page-the-untold-story-2014-4?IR=T

118 "Wo tut sich was am Bau," in *brand eins*, April 2016.

119 https://buildingradar.com/

120 *The Economist*, July 25, 2015.

121 *The Big Bang Theory*, season 2, ep. 13, "The Friendship Algorithm," https://www.youtube.com/watch?v=k0xgjUhEG3U

122 Chris Anderson, "The Man Who Makes the Future: *Wired* Icon Marc Andreessen," in *Wired*, April 24, 2012, http://www.wired.com/2012/04/ff_andreessen/

123 https://www.brainyquote.com/quotes/marc_andreessen_529636

124 *The Economist*, July 25, 2015.

125 Elon Musk, "All Our Patent Are Belong To You," June 12, 2014, https://www.teslamotors.com/blog/all-our-patent-are-belong-you

126 Christoph Keese, *Silicon Valley*, 2014, p. 100.

127 http://ovgrealestate.de/project-development/the-edge

128 Evelyn Grunau, "Ron Bakker on the Edge," in *TEDxAmsterdam*, July 16, 2015, http://tedx.amsterdam/2015/07/ron-bakker-on-the-edge/

129 Viktor Frankl, *Man's Search for Meaning*, 1946.

130 For LinkedIn, see https://press.linkedin.com/about-linkedin; for Google,

see https://www.google.com/intl/en/about/our-company/; for Huawei, see http://www.huawei.com/better-connected-world/en/huawei-bcw.html; for Sony, see https://www.sony.net/SonyInfo/; for Starbucks, see https://www. starbucks.com/about-us/company-information/mission-statement; for Hilti, see https://www.hilti.group/content/hilti/CP/XX/en/company/corporate-information/Strategy/core-purpose-and-values.html

131 Rita J. King, "Designing a Delicious Culture: The Tonight Show and Ben & Jerry's," February 23, 2015, https://www.linkedin.com/pulse/learning-org-design-from-tonight-show-ben-jerrys-rita-j-king

132 Katherine Martinko, "Ben & Jerry's now sourcing Fairtrade ingredients for all ice cream flavors", TreeHugger, April 13, 2015, http://www.treehugger. com/corporate-responsibility/ben-jerrys-now-sourcing-fairtrade-ingredients-all-ice-cream-flavors. html

133 Philipp Lichterbeck, Maren Peters, "Anti-Falten-Cremes sind Lügen," in *Das Sonntags- Magazin des Tagesspiegels*, no. 19,518, April 15, 2007, http://www. philipp-lichterbeck.com/wp-content/uploads/2007/04/Anita_Roddick.pdf

134 See http://www.salesforce.org/pledge-1

135 For a list of companies participating in Pledge 1%, see http://www.pledge-1percent.org/pledged.html.

136 Peter Senge, *The Fifth Discipline: The Art and Practice of the Learning Organization*, 1990. p. 66.

137 Philip Jodidio, "Five Works by Zaha Hadid," November 18, 2009, http:// www.architectureweek.com/2009/1118/design_1-1.html

138 Catherine Slessor, "2005 June: 'Top Gear'—BMW Central Building by Zaha Hadid, Leipzig, Germany," in *The Architectural Review*, August 9, 2011, https://www.architectural-review.com/buildings/2005-june-top-gear-bmw-central-building-by-zaha-hadid-leipzig-germany/8611830.article

139 Helmut Becker, *Phänomen Toyota, Erfolgsfaktor Ethik,* 2006.

140 Ed Catmull, Amy Wallace, *Creativity Inc.: Overcoming the Unseen Forces That Stand in the Way of True Inspiration*, 2014, p. 137.

141 Ibid., p. 138.

142 Ibid.

143 "Spotify Engineering Culture – part 1," https://vimeo.com/85490944

144 These examples are inspired by Brian J. Robertson, *Holocracy*, 2015.

145 Heiko Zwirner, "Von der Amöbe lernen," *brand eins wissen*, no. 08/0, http://www.brandeins.de/wissen/mck-wissen/menschen/von-der-amoebe-lernen/

146 Hans-Christian Riekhof (ed.), *Strategien der Personalentwicklung*, 1992, p. 248.

147 Suzanne Choney, "The responsive organization," in *Microsoft News Center*, http://news.microsoft.com/features/the-responsive-organization/#sm.00 001lz7gj14kxfe0tjfm7og21ydl

148 See the model of behavior developed in Lutz von Rosenstiel, Walter Molt, Bruno Rüttinger, *Organisationspsychologie*, 2005, p. 259.

149 http://www.ikea.com/ms/en_US/this-is-ikea/company-information/index.html

150 Peter Drucker, *The Essential Drucker: The Best of Sixty Years of Peter Drucker's Essential Writings on Management*, 2005, p. 20.

151 Stephen Eckett, *500 of the Most Witty, Acerbic and Erudite Things Ever Said About Money*, 2002.

152 Simon Sinek, "How great leaders inspire action," TED Talk, 2009, https://www.ted.com/talks/simon_sinek_how_great_leaders_inspire_action

153 Richard Branson, "Why all businesses should ask themselves 'why?'", https://www.virgin.com/richard-branson/why-all-businesses-should-ask-themselves-why

154 Claudine Beaumont, "Bill Gates's dream: A computer in every home," in *The Telegraph*, June 26, 2008, http://www.telegraph.co.uk/technology/3357701/Bill-Gatess-dream-A-computer-in-every-home.html

155 Steven A. Ballmer, "Shareholder Letter," 2013, http://www.microsoft.com/investor/reports/ar13/shareholder-letter/index.html

156 Andrea Nagy Smith, "What was Polaroid thinking?", in *Yale Insights*, November 4, 2009, http://insights.som.yale.edu/insights/what-was-polaroid-thinking

157 http://www.bmwstartupgarage.com/

158 Peter Drucker, *Management: Tasks, Responsibilities, Practices*, 1973.

159 RSA Animate, "Drive: The surprising truth about what motivates us," https://www.youtube.com/watch?v=u6XAPnuFjJc

160 Marcus Raitner, "Objectives and Key Results: Agil Ziele setzen," https://fuehrung-erfahren.de/2017/11/objectives-and-key-results-agil-ziele-setzen/

161 Cf. the idea of "Radical Candor," http://rstround.com/review/radical-candor-the-surprising-secret-to-being-a-good-boss/

162 Britta Domke, "Meetings sind für Führungskräfte Zeitfresser Nummer eins," in *Handelsblatt Online*, November 23, 2000, http://www.handelsblatt.com/archiv/meetings-sind-fuer-fuehrungskraefte-zeitfresser-nummer-eins/2020156.html.

163 Ferdinand Knauß, "Meetings machen krank," in *Die Zeit*, June 5, 2013, http://www.zeit.de/karriere/beruf/2013-05/meetings-stress-kommunikation.

164 Peter Drucker, *Management: Tasks, Responsibilities, Practices*, 1973, p. 472.

Index

Wladimir Klitschko, Stefanie Bilen
Challenge Management
What managers can learn
from the top athlete

2018. 208 pages

Also available as E-Book

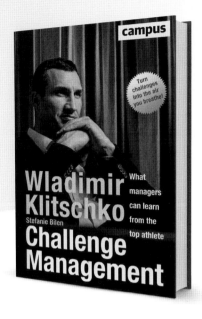

Like no other professional athlete, Dr. Wladimir Klitschko took care of his career outside the world of competitive sports while he still was an active boxer. He founded K2 Promotions, the KLITSCHKO Foundation, and the KLITSCHKO Management Group. In 2016 he even created a degree program at the prestigious University of St. Gallen in Switzerland, in which he teaches the basics of Self- and Challenge Management. KLITSCHKO Ventures, the holding company in which all his business activities are incorporated, followed. Dr. Wladimir Klitschko knows that a professional athlete has many skills from which the world of business can profit. It is his special talent to regard problems as challenges and accept them as a part of life. In this book, he finally explains how he does it. Now it's your turn to use his methods to make your business succeed, to master your personal challenges, and to take charge of your work and life!

campus.de

Frankfurt. New York

Sebastian Purps-Pardigol
Leading with the Brain
The 7 Neurobiological Factors
to Boost Employee Satisfaction
and Business Results

2016. 207 pages

Also available as E-Book

How do businesses inspire their employees so deeply that they will grow beyond themselves to achieve mutual success? Sebastian Purps-Pardigol has figured it out. Based on insights from brain research, psychology, behavioral economics, and 150 interviews with employees and CEOs, he has devised a new, innovative approach to the meaning of leadership today and what makes businesses unbeatable.
He presents seven factors business leaders should utilize to make their workforce feel more satisfied and increase the overall health and wellbeing of staff. In every business, there are hidden energies leaders cannot force their employees to use, but they can unleash these energies by leading in a human-centered way. Leading with the Brain is a fascinating and informative symbiosis of science and management.

campus.de

Frankfurt. New York

Fredmund Malik
Managing Performing Living
Effective Management
for a New World

2015. 405 pages

Also available as E-Book

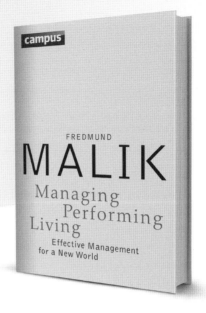

»Managing Performing Living« is a classic in the field of management. Fredmund Malik reveals everything that all executives and experts in leading positions need to know, anytime and anywhere. He provides readers with the universal principles, tasks and tools of effective management and self-management. His book ranks among the 100 best business books of all times. The new, completely revised and updated edition is tailored to a new generation of managers, to whom effectiveness is the key to success. It shows the way to turn knowledge, personal strengths, talent, creativity and innovative thinking into results. »Managing Performing Living« helps readers to cope with the »Great Transformation21«, as Malik calls the ongoing centennial change in business and society. It is a book on how to create functioning organizations in a viable society.

campus.de

campus

Frankfurt. New York